Ivy Global

SSAT
PRACTICE
EDITION 2.0

IVY GLOBAL, NEW YORK

*SSAT is a registered trademark of the Secondary School Admission Test Board which is not affiliated with and does not endorse this product.

SSAT Practice, Edition 2.0

This publication was written and edited by the team at Ivy Global.

Editor-in-Chief: Laurel Perkins
Layout Editor: Sacha Azor
Producers: Lloyd Min and Junho Suh

Contributors: Alexandra Candib, Isabel Carlin, Corwin Henville, Lei Huang, Mark Mendola, Sarah Pike, Yolanda Song, and Isabel Villeneuve

About Ivy Global

Ivy Global is a pioneering education company that provides a wide range of educational services.

E-mail: info@ivyglobal.com
Website: http://www.ivyglobal.com

Copyright 2017 by Ivy Global. All rights reserved.

Contents

Introduction
How to Use this Book 3

About the SSAT 5

Test-Taking Strategies
Approaching the SSAT 13

Practice Tests
Practice Test 1: Middle Level 29

Practice Test 2: Middle Level 75

Practice Test 3: Upper Level 123

Practice Test 4: Upper Level 173

Answers and Scoring
Practice Test 1: Middle Level 223

Practice Test 2: Middle Level 229

Practice Test 3: Upper Level 235

Practice Test 4: Upper Level 241

Introduction
Chapter 1

Section 1
How to Use this Book

Welcome, students and parents! This book is intended for students preparing for the Verbal, Reading, and Writing sections of the Middle or Upper Level Secondary School Admission Test (SSAT). For students applying to many top private and independent schools in North America, the SSAT is a crucial and sometimes daunting step in the admissions process. By leading you step-by-step through the fundamental content and most effective strategies for the SSAT, Ivy Global will help you build your confidence and maximize your score on this important exam.

This book is right for you if:

- you are applying to a private or independent school that requires the SSAT for admission
- you will be in Grades 5-7 (Middle Level) or 8-11 (Upper Level) when you write the SSAT
- you would like to practice for the SSAT exam using full-length practice tests under simulated testing conditions
- you are a parent, family member, or tutor looking for new ways to help your Middle or Upper-Level SSAT student

Ivy Global's *SSAT Practice* provides four full-length exams to help students practice for the SSAT under simulated testing conditions. This book includes:

- an up-to-date introduction to the SSAT's administration, format, and scoring practices
- instructions for taking a full-length practice test for the SSAT under simulated testing conditions
- 2 full-length practice tests for the SSAT Middle Level
- 2 full-length practice tests for the SSAT Upper Level
- detailed scoring instructions for each exam

Work through the exams that are appropriate to your level. After you have finished an exam, take time to assess your strengths and weaknesses. Then, spend some time reviewing the concepts you found challenging before you test yourself again.

To get started, continue reading for an overview of the SSAT and some general test-taking advice. Good luck in this exciting new step for your education!

Section 2
About the SSAT

The **SSAT (Secondary School Admission Test)** is a standardized test administered to students in grades 3-11 to help determine placement into certain private and independent schools. Many secondary schools worldwide use the SSAT as an integral part of their admissions process. The SSAT is owned, published, and developed by the Secondary School Admission Test Board. All tests are printed in English.

You will register for one of three SSAT tests, depending on your grade level:
- The **Elementary Level** exam is for students currently in grades 3-4.
- The **Middle Level** exam (formerly Lower Level) is for students currently in grades 5-7.
- The **Upper Level** exam is for students currently in grades 8-11.

All levels have the same basic format but vary in difficulty and length. The Elementary Level is shorter than the Middle and Upper Levels.

When is the Test Administered?

The SSAT is administered at national test centers on "**Standard**" dates eight times during the academic year. In some locations, regional private schools and organizations also have the option of administering the test independently on non-standard dates. These independent dates are called "**Flex**" test dates, and they are listed by region on the SSAT website at www.ssat.org. It does not matter whether you take the exam on a Standard or Flex test date if both are offered in your location.

How Many Times Can I Take the Test?

In most locations, a student can register for a Standard test as often as desired, up to eight times per academic year. However, a student can only register for a Flex test once per academic year. For students applying to schools in Ontario, the Ontario Testing Consortium allows students to register for only one SSAT test per academic year. Any subsequent attempts to take the exam will be considered invalid and will not be reported to schools.

How Do I Register?

The easiest and fastest way to register is to complete the **online application**. Visit www.ssat.org to register for an exam in your location. The other alternative is to mail or fax a completed form to SSAT by the regular registration deadline.

> Make sure to print off and keep the **Admission Ticket** that is obtainable only after SSAT has received and processed your registration and payment. This ticket both serves as a confirmation for your test registration, and includes important details of your pending test: date, location of scheduled test, specific instructions regarding taking the SSAT, and your list of schools and consultants chosen to receive your SSAT scores.

What is the Format of the SSAT?

The SSAT consists of three main sections (**Verbal**, **Math**, and **Reading**), plus a **Writing Sample** that either takes the form of a creative writing assignment or an essay. The format of the test differs based on the level of the exam:

Elementary Level			
Section	Questions	Length	Topics Covered
Math	30 questions	30 min	Arithmetic, geometry, word problems
Verbal	30 questions	20 min	Vocabulary: synonyms and analogies
		15-minute break	
Reading	28 questions	30 min	Short passages: fiction, non-fiction, poetry
Writing	1 prompt	15 min	Creative writing assignment (not scored)
		Total testing time: 1 hour, 50 minutes	

Middle and Upper Levels			
Section	Questions	Length	Topics Covered
Writing	One prompt	25 min	Creative writing assignment or essay (not scored)
5-minute break			
Math I	25 questions	30 min	Arithmetic, algebra, geometry, word problems
Reading	40 questions	40 min	Short passages: fiction, non-fiction, poetry
10-minute break			
Verbal	60 questions	30 min	Vocabulary: synonyms and analogies
Math II	25 questions	30 min	Arithmetic, algebra, geometry, word problems
Experimental Section	16 questions	15 min	Varies: this section is testing out questions for upcoming years and is not scored
Total testing time: 3 hours, 5 minutes			

Except for the Writing Sample, all questions are **multiple choice** (A) to (E). You are not allowed to use calculators, rulers, dictionaries, or other aids during the exam.

How is the SSAT Scored?

All of the multiple-choice questions on the SSAT are equal in value, and your **raw score** for these sections is calculated as follows:

- One mark is given for every question answered correctly.
- $\frac{1}{4}$ mark is deducted for every question answered incorrectly.
- No marks are awarded or deducted for questions left blank.

Therefore, your raw score is the number of questions you answer correctly subtracted by one quarter point for each question you answer incorrectly.

Your raw score is then converted into a **scaled score** for each section (Verbal, Math, and Reading) that represents how well you did in comparison to the other students taking the same exam:

- Elementary Level scaled score: 300-600 for each section, 900-1800 total
- Middle Level scaled score: 440-710 for each section, 1320-2130 total
- Upper Level scaled score: 500-800 for each section, 1500-2400 total

The **Writing Sample** is not scored, but is sent to the schools you are applying to as a sample of your writing skills. Admissions officers may use your essay or story to evaluate your writing ability when they are making admissions decisions.

The **Experimental Section** on the Middle and Upper Levels is the SSAT's method of testing out new questions for upcoming years. The section is not scored, but students should try to complete it to the best of their ability. The section may include any mixture of Verbal, Reading, or Math questions.

Scores are released to families and to the schools that families have designated as recipients within two weeks after the test date. Schools receive a printed report by mail and an electronic copy online. Families receive an electronic copy and can request a printed report for an extra fee. You may designate certain schools as recipients during registration, or at any time before or after testing through your online account at www.ssat.org.

What are the SSAT Percentiles?

The SSAT score report also provides **SSAT percentile** rankings for each category, comparing your performance to that of other students in the same grade who have taken the test in the past three years. If you score in the 60th percentile, this means you scored higher than 60% of other students in your grade taking the exam.

These percentile rankings provide a more accurate way of evaluating student performance at each grade level. However, the SSAT percentiles only compare your score to those of other students who have taken the SSAT, and these tend to be very high-achieving students. Students should not be discouraged if their percentile rankings appear low.

Because the Elementary Level exam was first administered in 2012, percentile data for this test has not yet been released.

	Median Scores (SSAT 50th Percentile)			
	Grade	Reading	Verbal	Quantitative
Middle Level	5	585	590	587
	6	603	610	611
	7	628	635	635
Upper Level	8	647	660	676
	9	653	667	699
	10	659	670	705
	11	647	656	704

The SSAT also publishes an Estimated National Percentile Ranking for test takers in grades 5-9, which provides an estimated comparison of student performance against the entire national student population, not just the set of students taking the SSAT. The test also provides a projected SAT score for test-takers in grades 7-10.

How Do Schools Use the SSAT?

Schools use the SSAT as one way to assess potential applicants, but it is by no means the only tool that they are using. Schools also pay very close attention to the rest of the student's application—academic record, teacher recommendations, extracurricular activities, writing samples, and interviews—in order to determine which students might be the best fit for their program. The personal components of a student's application give schools a lot more information about the student's personality and potential contributions to the school's overall community. Different schools place a different amount of importance on SSAT and other test scores within this process, and admissions offices are good places to find how much your schools of interest will weight the SSAT.

Test-Taking Strategies
Chapter 2

Section 1
Approaching the SSAT

Before you review the content covered on the SSAT, you need to focus on *how* you take the SSAT. If you approach the SSAT *thoughtfully* and *strategically*, you will avoid common traps and tricks planted in the SSAT by the test makers. Think of the SSAT as a timed maze—you need to make every turn cleverly and quickly so that you avoid getting stuck at a dead end with no time to spare.

In this section, you will learn about the SSAT's format and structure; this awareness will help you avoid any surprises or shocks on test day. A very predictable exam, the SSAT will seem less challenging once you understand what it looks like and how it works. By learning strategies and techniques for best test-taking practice, you will discover how to work as quickly and intelligently as possible. Once you know what to expect, you can refine your knowledge of the content tested on the SSAT, such as the verbal and math skills that are based on your grade level in school.

This section on SSAT strategies will answer your major questions:

- How does the SSAT differ from a test you take in school?
- What preparation strategies can you learn before you take the SSAT?
- What strategies can you learn to use during the SSAT?
- How can you manage stress before and during the SSAT?

In the process of answering your big questions, this section will also highlight key facts about smart test-taking:

- Your answer choice matters—your process does not. Grid your answer choices correctly and carefully to earn points. You have a set amount of time per section, so spend it wisely.
- The SSAT's format and directions do not change, so learn them now.
- All questions have the same value.
- Each level of the SSAT corresponds to a range of grades, and score expectations differ based on your grade level.
- Identify your areas of strength and weakness, and review any content that feels unfamiliar.

- Apply universal strategies—prediction-making, Process of Elimination, back-solving, and educated guessing—to the multiple-choice sections.
- Stay calm and be confident in your abilities as you prepare for and take the SSAT.

How Does the SSAT Differ from a Test You Take in School?
Part 1

The SSAT differs from assessments you take in school in four major ways:
1. It is not concerned with the process behind your answers. Your answer is either right or wrong; there is no partial credit.
2. You have a set amount of time per section (and for the exam as a whole).
3. It is divided into three levels that correspond to three grade ranges of students.
4. It is extremely predictable given that its format, structure, and directions never vary.

No Partial Credit

At this point in your school career, you have probably heard your teacher remark, "Be sure to show your work on the test!" You are most likely familiar with almost every teacher's policy of "No work, no credit." However, the SSAT completely ignores this guideline. The machine that grades your exam does not care that you penciled brilliant logic in the margins of the test booklet—the machine only looks at your gridded answer choice. Your answer choice is either right or wrong; **there is no partial credit**.

Set Amount of Time

You have a **set amount of time per section**, so spend it wisely. The SSAT test proctors will never award you extra time after a test section has ended because you spent half of one section struggling valiantly on a single problem. Instead, you must learn to work within each section's time constraints.

You also must view the questions as equal because **each question is worth one point**. Even though some questions are more challenging than others, they all carry the same weight. Rather than dwell on a problem, you should skip it, work through the rest of the section, and come back to it if you have time.

Three Levels

There are three levels of the SSAT—Elementary, Middle, and Upper—each of which is administered to a specific range of students. The Elementary Level is given to students in grades 3 and 4; the Middle Level is given to students in grades 5, 6, and 7; and the Upper Level is given to students in grades 8, 9, 10, and 11. While you might be used to taking tests in school that are completely tailored to your grade, the SSAT is different: each test level covers content from a specific range of grade levels.

Score expectations differ based on your grade level. You are not expected to answer as many questions correctly on a Middle Level exam if you are only in fifth grade. Conversely, if you are in seventh grade, you are expected to answer the most questions correctly on the Middle Level exam because you are one of the oldest students taking that exam.

Standard Format

The SSAT is, by definition, a **standardized test**, which means that its format and directions are standard and predictable. While your teachers might change formats and directions for every assessment they administer, you can expect to see the same format and directions on every SSAT.

What Preparation Strategies Can You Learn Before You Take the SSAT?
Part 2

Now that you are familiar with how the SSAT differs from the tests you take in school, you are ready to learn some test tips. You can prepare for the SSAT by following these three steps:

- Learn the format and directions of the test.
- Identify your areas of strength and weakness.
- Create a study schedule to review and practice test content.

Learn the Format and Directions

The structure of the SSAT is entirely predictable, so learn this now. Rather than wasting precious time reading the directions and understanding the format on test day, take the time now to familiarize yourself with the test's format and directions.

Refer to the tables on page 6 and 7 for an overview of the SSAT's format. Specific directions for the Verbal, Reading, and Writing sections can be found in Ivy Global's *SSAT English*. Specific directions for the math section can be found in Ivy Global's *SSAT Math*.

Identify Your Strengths and Weaknesses

To determine your areas of strength and weakness and identify which concepts you need to review, take a full-length, accurate practice exam to serve as a diagnostic test. Four full-length practice exams can be found in this book: two for the Middle Level and two for the Upper Level.

Make sure you simulate test day conditions by timing yourself. Then, check your answers against the correct answers. Write down how many questions you missed in each section, and note the topics or types of questions you found most challenging (e.g. analogies, fiction passages, geometry, or data analysis). What was hard about the test? What did you feel good about? Did you leave a lot of questions blank because of timing issues, or did you leave questions blank because you did not know how to solve them? Reflecting on these questions, in addition to looking at your score breakdown, will help you determine your strengths, weaknesses, and areas for improvement.

Create a Study Schedule

After determining your areas of strength and weakness, create a study plan and schedule for your SSAT preparation to review content. Work backward from your test date until you arrive at your starting point for studying. The number of weeks you have until your exam will determine how much time you can (and should) devote to your preparation. Remember, practice is the most important thing!

To begin, try using this sample study plan as a model for your own personalized study schedule.

Sample Study Plan

My test date is: _____.

I have _____ weeks to study. I will make an effort to study _____ minutes/hours every day/week, and I will set aside extra time on _____ to take timed sections.

I plan to take _____ full-length tests between now and my test date. I will study for _____ weeks and then take a practice test. My goal for this test is to improve my score in the following specific areas:

_____

_____

_____

_____

_____

_____

_____

_____

_____

_____

If I do not make this goal, then I will spend more time studying.

| Study Schedule |||||
Date	Plan of Study	Time Allotted	Time Spent	Goal Reached?
1/1	Learn 5 words and review perimeter of polygons	1 hour	44 minutes	Yes, I know 5 new words and can calculate perimeter!
1/3	Learn 5 words and review area of triangles	1 hour	1 hour	I know 5 new words, but I'm still confused about the area of triangles. I'll review this again next time and ask a teacher, tutor, or parent for help.

Approaching the SSAT

What Strategies Can You Learn to Use During the Test?
Part 3

Once you have grown accustomed to the SSAT through practice, you are ready to learn strategies to use during the SSAT. The following points will prepare you to take the test as cleverly and efficiently as possible:

- Grid your answer choices correctly and carefully.
- Pace yourself to manage your time effectively.
- Learn a strategic approach for multiple-choice questions.

Gridding Answer Choices

For the Middle and Upper Level exams, you must enter your answers on a separate answer sheet. In school you probably take tests that, for the most part, do not ask you to transfer your answers to a separate sheet. However, the SSAT streamlines the grading process by only reviewing your answer sheet. You must grid in your multiple-choice answers onto this sheet using an HB pencil to fill in the circle that corresponds to your answer. This sheet is scanned and scored by a highly sensitive computer. You will also write your Writing Sample on separate lined pages of this answer sheet.

Since you have to take an additional step to record your answers, it is important that you avoid making gridding mistakes. Sadly, many students get confused and mismark their answer sheets. Remember, even if you arrive at the right answer, it is only correct and counted in your favor if you grid correctly on your answer sheet.

To grid correctly and carefully to maximize your points, consider the following tips:

Keep your answer sheet neat. Since your answer sheet is graded by a machine, your score is calculated based on what your marks look like. The machine cannot know what you really meant if you picked the wrong bubble. Stray marks can harm your score, especially if you darken the correct answer but accidentally make a mark that confuses the machine! Avoid this and other errors by consulting the following image, which shows the difference between answers that are properly shaded and those that are not.

1. Ⓐ Ⓑ Ⓒ ⓓ Ⓔ   ✗   Answer 1 is wrong because no answer is selected and there are stray marks.

2. Ⓐ Ⓑ Ⓒ Ⓓ Ⓔ   ✗   Answer 2 is neither right nor wrong because it was left blank.

3. Ⓐ Ⓑ ⓒ ⓓ Ⓔ   ✗   Answer 3 is wrong because two answers have been selected.

4. Ⓐ ● Ⓒ ● Ⓔ   ✗   Answer 4 is wrong because two answers have been selected.

5. Ⓐ Ⓑ Ⓒ Ⓓ ⓧ   ✗   Answer 5 is wrong because choice (E) has not been darkened properly and there are stray marks.

6. ● Ⓑ Ⓒ Ⓓ Ⓔ   ✓   Answer 6 is right because choice (A) has been darkened properly.

Train yourself to **circle your answer choice in your test booklet**. If you have time to go back and check your answers, you can easily check your circled answers against your gridded ones.

You should also **create a system for marking questions that you skipped** or that you found confusing (see the next section for more information about skipping around). Try circling those question numbers only in your test booklet so that you can find them if you want to solve them later or check your work. Be aware of these questions when gridding answers on your answer sheet.

Finally, **grid your answers in batches of four, five, or six answer choices.** That way, you do not have to go back and forth between your test booklet and your answer sheet every minute. If you choose to use this strategy, keep an eye on the clock—you do not want to get to the end of the section and find you have not gridded any answers. Depending on how much time you have left to check your work (if you happen to finish early), you can either review every problem or spot-check a series of questions on your answer sheet against your test booklet.

Time Management (Pacing)

Manage your time effectively to boost your score. Just as effective gridding contributes to time management, other strategies enable you to work efficiently and maximize the number of problems you answer. Specifically, skipping questions is particularly important because you need to learn to keep moving on the exam rather than wasting too much time on any single question.

You can skip questions within each section of the SSAT; the freedom to skip questions is helpful since each question is worth only one point. If you are stuck on a problem, you should move on after a minute or two and try to answer another problem. It makes more sense to answer as many questions as possible (and get as many points as possible) rather than spending all your time on one question. If you come across a question you want to skip, mark it in your question booklet (by circling it, underlining it, etc.) and move to the next question; just be sure to skip the corresponding number on your answer sheet if you choose to skip questions. Remember not to make any stray marks on your answer sheet.

Approaching the SSAT

There is a benefit to skipping questions. By moving quickly through each question of the section, you will ensure that: 1) you see every question in the section; 2) you gain points on questions that are easy for you; 3) you return to more challenging problems and hopefully answer as many as you can with your remaining time. It is also important to note that you might not be able to answer several questions in each section if you are on the younger end of the testing group for your particular test level. In that case, you should skip those questions unless you can eliminate one or more answer choices. Also, think about the value of skipping in terms of the guessing penalty. If you cannot make a clever guess on a hard problem, then you should skip it and move on because choosing a random answer will most likely cause you to lose one quarter of a point.

Follow this step-by-step process to decide when to skip questions:
1. Look through the section and answer the questions that are easy for you first. Circle any questions that you are not sure about or seem harder.
2. After answering all the easier questions, go back to the questions you have circled and spend some time working on ones that you think you might be able to solve.
3. Skip any questions that you have no idea how to solve.

Continue reading for more detailed information about the guessing penalty and guessing strategies.

Strategies for Multiple-Choice Questions

Apply universal strategies—prediction-making, Process of Elimination, back-solving, and educated guessing—to the multiple-choice sections. To illustrate the value of these strategies, read through the following example of a synonym question from the Verbal Section:

Example
HAPPY:
(A) delighted
(B) unhappy
(C) crazy
(D) nice
(E) depressed

Answer: (A). "Delighted" is the correct answer because it is the word that most nearly means "happy."

Regardless of whether the answer choices are easy, difficult, or somewhere in between, you can use certain tricks and tips to your advantage. To approach SSAT questions effectively, you need to step into the test makers' minds and learn to use their traps against them.

Make predictions. When you see a question, try to come up with an answer on your own before looking at the answer choices. You can literally cover the answer choices with your hand so that you must rely on your own intelligence to predict an answer instead of being swayed by answer choices that you see. If you look at the answer choices first, you might be tempted to circle a choice without thinking about the other options and what the question is asking you. Instead, make a prediction so that you understand the question fully and get a clear sense of what to look for in the answers. In the synonym example above, you could predict that a possible synonym for "happy" would be something like "glad."

Use the **Process of Elimination**. For each multiple-choice question, the answer is always right in front of you. To narrow down your answer choices, actively identify obviously incorrect answers and eliminate them. Even if you can eliminate just one answer, you will set yourself up for better odds if you decide to guess. For the synonym example above, test your prediction of "glad" against the answer choices and immediately eliminate "unhappy" and "depressed" since they are nearly opposite in meaning. You can also probably eliminate "crazy" and "nice" since those words do not match your prediction as well as "delighted," which is the correct answer.

Try back-solving. This strategy is most useful on the math sections, especially when you are given a complicated, multi-step word problem. Instead of writing an equation, try plugging in the answer choices to the word problem. Take a look at the following question:

Example
Catherine has a basket of candy. On Monday, she eats ½ of all the candy. On Tuesday, she eats 2 pieces. On Wednesday, she eats twice the amount of candy that she consumed on Tuesday. If she only has 4 pieces left on Thursday, how many pieces did she initially have?

(A) 12
(B) 14
(C) 16
(D) 20
(E) 22

To use back-solving, start with answer choice (C) and plug it into the word problem. If (C) is the correct answer, you are done. If not, you will then know whether you should test (B) or (D). On the SSAT, numerical answer options are always listed in either ascending or descending order, from least to greatest or from greatest to least, meaning that even if (C) is incorrect, you will then be able to identify whether your answer should be larger or smaller than (C); you can then test (B) or (D) accordingly.

When we start with 16 pieces of candy, we subtract 8 on Monday, then 4 more for Tuesday, and then 2 more for Wednesday. By Thursday, Catherine only has two pieces of candy left, which is less than the amount we wanted. Therefore, we know our answer has to be bigger, so we eliminate choices (A), (B), and (C) and try (D), which works.

(*Fun Fact:* If you think about it, you will only ever have to plug in three answer choices at most to determine the right answer.)

Use educated guessing. Before taking any test, it is important to understand the test's grading rules for correct answers, incorrect answers, and blank answers. The SSAT has a **wrong-answer penalty** for all three levels of the test, which means:

- You lose one quarter of a point from your total score for each question you answer incorrectly.
- You receive one point for every question you answer correctly.
- If you leave a question blank, you do not lose points—but you do not gain points either (so your score will not reach the highest possible range).

The SSAT's penalty is often referred to as a guessing penalty since its purpose is to discourage random guessing. If you did not lose points for guessing, then you could possibly pick the same answer choice for an entire section and get twenty percent of the questions—or more—correct. Thus, the guessing penalty is important because it makes sure your score reflects your abilities rather than your luck when guessing.

Guessing cleverly can certainly improve your score. If you can rule out one or two choices for a tricky question, then you should guess because your chances for guessing correctly are above average. However, if you cannot eliminate any of the answer choices, then guessing is not worth the risk of a quarter-point penalty. In that case, leave the answer blank and move on quickly to gain points on other questions.

Armed with these strategies, you might feel that SSAT is starting to look more manageable because you now have shortcuts that will help you navigate the maze of questions quickly and cleverly.

Take a look at this example to practice using the strategies you just read about.

Example
Doll is to toy as pasta is to (A) mall (B) Italy (C) America (D) dessert (E) food

1. Assess the question and recognize what it is testing. In this case, the question tests whether you can complete the analogy.
2. Make a prediction. A doll is a type of toy, so pasta must be a type of something. How about "dinner"?

3. Look for inaccurate answer choices and eliminate them. "Mall" does not make sense. "Italy" and "America" both make pasta, but they are not examples of food or dinner. Dessert is a type of food, but pasta is not a dessert. "Food" is the only possible answer in this case.
4. Make an educated guess, or choose the best answer if you feel confident about it. Since you made a fantastic prediction and used Process of Elimination, you only have one choice left: (E). "Food" is the correct answer—you just earned yourself a point!

How Can You Manage Your Stress?
Part 4

It is natural to be nervous leading up to your exam. However, if that feeling starts to become overwhelming, here are some strategies that you can use. Many of these suggestions are good ideas to use in everyday life, but they become especially important in the final week before your test and on test day itself.

- **Relax and slow down.** To center yourself and ease your nerves, take a big, deep breath. Slowly inhale for a few seconds and then slowly exhale for a few seconds. Shut your eyes and relax. Stretch your arms, roll your neck gently, crack your knuckles—get in the zone of Zen! Continue to breathe deeply and slowly until you can literally feel your body calm down.
- **Picture your goals.** Close your eyes or just pause to reflect on what you want to achieve on test day. Visualize your success; acknowledge your former successes and abilities, and believe in yourself.
- **Break it down.** Instead of trying to study a whole section at once, break up your studying into small and manageable chunks. Outline your study goals before you start. For example, instead of trying to master the entire Reading Section at once, you might want to work on one type of passage at a time.
- **Sleep.** Make sure you get plenty of rest and sleep, especially the two nights leading up to your exam.
- **Fuel up.** Eat healthy, filling meals that fuel your brain. Also, drink lots of water to stay hydrated.
- **Take a break.** Put down the books and go play outside, read, listen to music, exercise, or talk to a trusted friend or family member. A good break can be just as restful as a nap. However, watching television will provide minimal relaxation.

On the night before the exam, study only lightly. Make a list of your three biggest fears and work on them, but don't try to learn anything new. Pick out what you are going to wear to the exam—try wearing layers in case the exam room is hotter or colder than you expect. Organize everything you need to bring, including your Admissions Ticket. Know where the test center is located and how long it will take to get there. Have a nutritious meal and get plenty of sleep!

On the morning of the exam, let your adrenaline kick in naturally. Eat a good breakfast and stay hydrated; your body needs fuel to endure the test. Bring along several pencils and a good eraser. Listen carefully to the test proctor's instructions and let the proctor know if you are left-handed so you can sit in an appropriate desk. Take a deep breath and remember: you are smart and accomplished! Believe in yourself and you will do just fine.

Practice Tests
Chapter 3

Middle Level
Practice Test 1

How to Take this Practice Test
Part 1

To simulate an accurate testing environment, sit at a desk in a quiet location free of distractions—no TV, computers, phones, music, or noise—and clear your desk of all materials except pencils and erasers. Remember that no calculators, rulers, protractors, dictionaries, or other aids are allowed on the SSAT.

Give yourself the following amounts of time for each section:

Section	Subject	Time Limit
	Writing	25 minutes
	5-minute break	
1	Math I	30 minutes
2	Reading	40 minutes
	5-minute break	
3	Verbal	30 minutes
4	Math II	30 minutes

Have an adult help you monitor your time, or use a stopwatch and time yourself. Only give yourself the allotted time for each section; put your pencil down when your time is up. Note: timing may be extended for students with diagnosed learning disabilities who apply for testing with accommodations.

Follow the instructions carefully. As you take your test, bubble your answers into the answer sheets provided. Use the test booklet as scratch paper for notes and calculations. Remember that you are not granted time at the end of a section to transfer your answers to the answer sheet, so you must do this as you go along.

When you are finished, check your answers against the answer keys provided. Then, score your exam using the directions at the end.

Be sure each mark completely fills the answer space.

Start with number 1 for each new section of the test. You may find more answer spaces than you need. If so, please leave them blank.

SECTION 1

1. Ⓐ Ⓑ Ⓒ Ⓓ Ⓔ	6. Ⓐ Ⓑ Ⓒ Ⓓ Ⓔ	11. Ⓐ Ⓑ Ⓒ Ⓓ Ⓔ	16. Ⓐ Ⓑ Ⓒ Ⓓ Ⓔ	21. Ⓐ Ⓑ Ⓒ Ⓓ Ⓔ
2. Ⓐ Ⓑ Ⓒ Ⓓ Ⓔ	7. Ⓐ Ⓑ Ⓒ Ⓓ Ⓔ	12. Ⓐ Ⓑ Ⓒ Ⓓ Ⓔ	17. Ⓐ Ⓑ Ⓒ Ⓓ Ⓔ	22. Ⓐ Ⓑ Ⓒ Ⓓ Ⓔ
3. Ⓐ Ⓑ Ⓒ Ⓓ Ⓔ	8. Ⓐ Ⓑ Ⓒ Ⓓ Ⓔ	13. Ⓐ Ⓑ Ⓒ Ⓓ Ⓔ	18. Ⓐ Ⓑ Ⓒ Ⓓ Ⓔ	23. Ⓐ Ⓑ Ⓒ Ⓓ Ⓔ
4. Ⓐ Ⓑ Ⓒ Ⓓ Ⓔ	9. Ⓐ Ⓑ Ⓒ Ⓓ Ⓔ	14. Ⓐ Ⓑ Ⓒ Ⓓ Ⓔ	19. Ⓐ Ⓑ Ⓒ Ⓓ Ⓔ	24. Ⓐ Ⓑ Ⓒ Ⓓ Ⓔ
5. Ⓐ Ⓑ Ⓒ Ⓓ Ⓔ	10. Ⓐ Ⓑ Ⓒ Ⓓ Ⓔ	15. Ⓐ Ⓑ Ⓒ Ⓓ Ⓔ	20. Ⓐ Ⓑ Ⓒ Ⓓ Ⓔ	25. Ⓐ Ⓑ Ⓒ Ⓓ Ⓔ

SECTION 2

1. Ⓐ Ⓑ Ⓒ Ⓓ Ⓔ	9. Ⓐ Ⓑ Ⓒ Ⓓ Ⓔ	17. Ⓐ Ⓑ Ⓒ Ⓓ Ⓔ	25. Ⓐ Ⓑ Ⓒ Ⓓ Ⓔ	33. Ⓐ Ⓑ Ⓒ Ⓓ Ⓔ
2. Ⓐ Ⓑ Ⓒ Ⓓ Ⓔ	10. Ⓐ Ⓑ Ⓒ Ⓓ Ⓔ	18. Ⓐ Ⓑ Ⓒ Ⓓ Ⓔ	26. Ⓐ Ⓑ Ⓒ Ⓓ Ⓔ	34. Ⓐ Ⓑ Ⓒ Ⓓ Ⓔ
3. Ⓐ Ⓑ Ⓒ Ⓓ Ⓔ	11. Ⓐ Ⓑ Ⓒ Ⓓ Ⓔ	19. Ⓐ Ⓑ Ⓒ Ⓓ Ⓔ	27. Ⓐ Ⓑ Ⓒ Ⓓ Ⓔ	35. Ⓐ Ⓑ Ⓒ Ⓓ Ⓔ
4. Ⓐ Ⓑ Ⓒ Ⓓ Ⓔ	12. Ⓐ Ⓑ Ⓒ Ⓓ Ⓔ	20. Ⓐ Ⓑ Ⓒ Ⓓ Ⓔ	28. Ⓐ Ⓑ Ⓒ Ⓓ Ⓔ	36. Ⓐ Ⓑ Ⓒ Ⓓ Ⓔ
5. Ⓐ Ⓑ Ⓒ Ⓓ Ⓔ	13. Ⓐ Ⓑ Ⓒ Ⓓ Ⓔ	21. Ⓐ Ⓑ Ⓒ Ⓓ Ⓔ	29. Ⓐ Ⓑ Ⓒ Ⓓ Ⓔ	37. Ⓐ Ⓑ Ⓒ Ⓓ Ⓔ
6. Ⓐ Ⓑ Ⓒ Ⓓ Ⓔ	14. Ⓐ Ⓑ Ⓒ Ⓓ Ⓔ	22. Ⓐ Ⓑ Ⓒ Ⓓ Ⓔ	30. Ⓐ Ⓑ Ⓒ Ⓓ Ⓔ	38. Ⓐ Ⓑ Ⓒ Ⓓ Ⓔ
7. Ⓐ Ⓑ Ⓒ Ⓓ Ⓔ	15. Ⓐ Ⓑ Ⓒ Ⓓ Ⓔ	23. Ⓐ Ⓑ Ⓒ Ⓓ Ⓔ	31. Ⓐ Ⓑ Ⓒ Ⓓ Ⓔ	39. Ⓐ Ⓑ Ⓒ Ⓓ Ⓔ
8. Ⓐ Ⓑ Ⓒ Ⓓ Ⓔ	16. Ⓐ Ⓑ Ⓒ Ⓓ Ⓔ	24. Ⓐ Ⓑ Ⓒ Ⓓ Ⓔ	32. Ⓐ Ⓑ Ⓒ Ⓓ Ⓔ	40. Ⓐ Ⓑ Ⓒ Ⓓ Ⓔ

SECTION 3

1. Ⓐ Ⓑ Ⓒ Ⓓ Ⓔ	13. Ⓐ Ⓑ Ⓒ Ⓓ Ⓔ	25. Ⓐ Ⓑ Ⓒ Ⓓ Ⓔ	37. Ⓐ Ⓑ Ⓒ Ⓓ Ⓔ	49. Ⓐ Ⓑ Ⓒ Ⓓ Ⓔ
2. Ⓐ Ⓑ Ⓒ Ⓓ Ⓔ	14. Ⓐ Ⓑ Ⓒ Ⓓ Ⓔ	26. Ⓐ Ⓑ Ⓒ Ⓓ Ⓔ	38. Ⓐ Ⓑ Ⓒ Ⓓ Ⓔ	50. Ⓐ Ⓑ Ⓒ Ⓓ Ⓔ
3. Ⓐ Ⓑ Ⓒ Ⓓ Ⓔ	15. Ⓐ Ⓑ Ⓒ Ⓓ Ⓔ	27. Ⓐ Ⓑ Ⓒ Ⓓ Ⓔ	39. Ⓐ Ⓑ Ⓒ Ⓓ Ⓔ	51. Ⓐ Ⓑ Ⓒ Ⓓ Ⓔ
4. Ⓐ Ⓑ Ⓒ Ⓓ Ⓔ	16. Ⓐ Ⓑ Ⓒ Ⓓ Ⓔ	28. Ⓐ Ⓑ Ⓒ Ⓓ Ⓔ	40. Ⓐ Ⓑ Ⓒ Ⓓ Ⓔ	52. Ⓐ Ⓑ Ⓒ Ⓓ Ⓔ
5. Ⓐ Ⓑ Ⓒ Ⓓ Ⓔ	17. Ⓐ Ⓑ Ⓒ Ⓓ Ⓔ	29. Ⓐ Ⓑ Ⓒ Ⓓ Ⓔ	41. Ⓐ Ⓑ Ⓒ Ⓓ Ⓔ	53. Ⓐ Ⓑ Ⓒ Ⓓ Ⓔ
6. Ⓐ Ⓑ Ⓒ Ⓓ Ⓔ	18. Ⓐ Ⓑ Ⓒ Ⓓ Ⓔ	30. Ⓐ Ⓑ Ⓒ Ⓓ Ⓔ	42. Ⓐ Ⓑ Ⓒ Ⓓ Ⓔ	54. Ⓐ Ⓑ Ⓒ Ⓓ Ⓔ
7. Ⓐ Ⓑ Ⓒ Ⓓ Ⓔ	19. Ⓐ Ⓑ Ⓒ Ⓓ Ⓔ	31. Ⓐ Ⓑ Ⓒ Ⓓ Ⓔ	43. Ⓐ Ⓑ Ⓒ Ⓓ Ⓔ	55. Ⓐ Ⓑ Ⓒ Ⓓ Ⓔ
8. Ⓐ Ⓑ Ⓒ Ⓓ Ⓔ	20. Ⓐ Ⓑ Ⓒ Ⓓ Ⓔ	32. Ⓐ Ⓑ Ⓒ Ⓓ Ⓔ	44. Ⓐ Ⓑ Ⓒ Ⓓ Ⓔ	56. Ⓐ Ⓑ Ⓒ Ⓓ Ⓔ
9. Ⓐ Ⓑ Ⓒ Ⓓ Ⓔ	21. Ⓐ Ⓑ Ⓒ Ⓓ Ⓔ	33. Ⓐ Ⓑ Ⓒ Ⓓ Ⓔ	45. Ⓐ Ⓑ Ⓒ Ⓓ Ⓔ	57. Ⓐ Ⓑ Ⓒ Ⓓ Ⓔ
10. Ⓐ Ⓑ Ⓒ Ⓓ Ⓔ	22. Ⓐ Ⓑ Ⓒ Ⓓ Ⓔ	34. Ⓐ Ⓑ Ⓒ Ⓓ Ⓔ	46. Ⓐ Ⓑ Ⓒ Ⓓ Ⓔ	58. Ⓐ Ⓑ Ⓒ Ⓓ Ⓔ
11. Ⓐ Ⓑ Ⓒ Ⓓ Ⓔ	23. Ⓐ Ⓑ Ⓒ Ⓓ Ⓔ	35. Ⓐ Ⓑ Ⓒ Ⓓ Ⓔ	47. Ⓐ Ⓑ Ⓒ Ⓓ Ⓔ	59. Ⓐ Ⓑ Ⓒ Ⓓ Ⓔ
12. Ⓐ Ⓑ Ⓒ Ⓓ Ⓔ	24. Ⓐ Ⓑ Ⓒ Ⓓ Ⓔ	36. Ⓐ Ⓑ Ⓒ Ⓓ Ⓔ	48. Ⓐ Ⓑ Ⓒ Ⓓ Ⓔ	60. Ⓐ Ⓑ Ⓒ Ⓓ Ⓔ

SECTION 4

1. Ⓐ Ⓑ Ⓒ Ⓓ Ⓔ	6. Ⓐ Ⓑ Ⓒ Ⓓ Ⓔ	11. Ⓐ Ⓑ Ⓒ Ⓓ Ⓔ	16. Ⓐ Ⓑ Ⓒ Ⓓ Ⓔ	21. Ⓐ Ⓑ Ⓒ Ⓓ Ⓔ
2. Ⓐ Ⓑ Ⓒ Ⓓ Ⓔ	7. Ⓐ Ⓑ Ⓒ Ⓓ Ⓔ	12. Ⓐ Ⓑ Ⓒ Ⓓ Ⓔ	17. Ⓐ Ⓑ Ⓒ Ⓓ Ⓔ	22. Ⓐ Ⓑ Ⓒ Ⓓ Ⓔ
3. Ⓐ Ⓑ Ⓒ Ⓓ Ⓔ	8. Ⓐ Ⓑ Ⓒ Ⓓ Ⓔ	13. Ⓐ Ⓑ Ⓒ Ⓓ Ⓔ	18. Ⓐ Ⓑ Ⓒ Ⓓ Ⓔ	23. Ⓐ Ⓑ Ⓒ Ⓓ Ⓔ
4. Ⓐ Ⓑ Ⓒ Ⓓ Ⓔ	9. Ⓐ Ⓑ Ⓒ Ⓓ Ⓔ	14. Ⓐ Ⓑ Ⓒ Ⓓ Ⓔ	19. Ⓐ Ⓑ Ⓒ Ⓓ Ⓔ	24. Ⓐ Ⓑ Ⓒ Ⓓ Ⓔ
5. Ⓐ Ⓑ Ⓒ Ⓓ Ⓔ	10. Ⓐ Ⓑ Ⓒ Ⓓ Ⓔ	15. Ⓐ Ⓑ Ⓒ Ⓓ Ⓔ	20. Ⓐ Ⓑ Ⓒ Ⓓ Ⓔ	25. Ⓐ Ⓑ Ⓒ Ⓓ Ⓔ

Writing Sample

Schools would like to get to know you better through a story you tell using one of the ideas below. Please choose the idea you find most interesting and write a story using the idea as your first sentence. Please fill in the circle next to the one you choose.

(A) I looked down and I saw ...

(B) They said it couldn't be done.

Use this page and the next page to complete your writing sample.

Continue on next page

SECTION 1
25 Questions

Following each problem in this section, there are five suggested answers. Work out each problem in your head or in the blank space provided at the right of the page. Then look at the five suggested answers and decide which one is best.

Note: Figures that accompany problems in this section are drawn as accurately as possible EXCEPT when it is stated in a specific problem that its figure is not drawn to scale.

Sample problem:

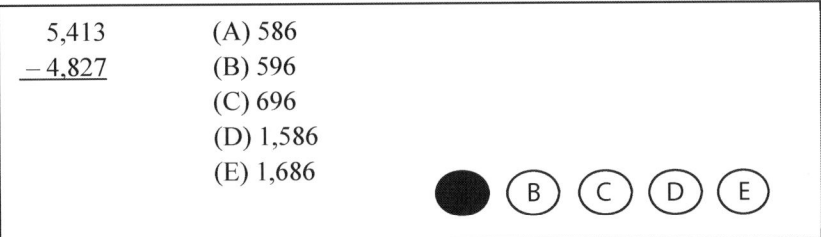

USE THIS SPACE FOR FIGURING.

1. Every year Juan goes swimming at least ten times. How many times will he go swimming in ten years?

    (A) at least one hundred times
    (B) fewer than one hundred times
    (C) at least one thousand times
    (D) fewer than ten times
    (E) exactly ten times

2. Suzie has 2 pencils, and Amy gives her 6 more. Then, Suzie loses 7 pencils. How many pencils does Suzie have now?

    (A) 1
    (B) 2
    (C) 3
    (D) 4
    (E) 5

GO ON TO THE NEXT PAGE.

Practice Test 1: Middle Level

3. $7 + 25/9 =$

(A) $9\frac{3}{9}$

(B) $9\frac{7}{9}$

(C) $10\frac{1}{3}$

(D) $10\frac{7}{9}$

(E) $11\frac{1}{3}$

4. If $4 \times 3 \times M = 0$, what is the value of M?

(A) 0

(B) $1/12$

(C) 1

(D) 7

(E) 12

5. Figure 1 shows a treasure map. To find the location of the hidden treasure, the instructions tell the reader to start at point X, then walk 7 units north. Then, the reader must walk 2.5 units east and 2 units south to arrive at the point where the treasure is hidden. Which point marks the location of the hidden treasure?

(A) A
(B) B
(C) C
(D) D
(E) E

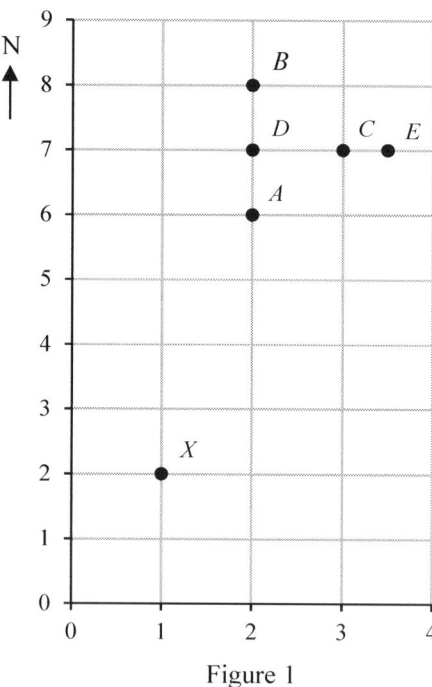

Figure 1

6. In the city of Townville, there are *C* cars, *T* tricycles, *B* bicycles, and one high-speed train called the Arrow that runs on sixteen wheels. The total number of wheels on all of these vehicles is equal to

   (A) $2C + 3T + 2B + 16$
   (B) $4C + 3B + 2T + A$
   (C) $2C + 3T + 2B + A$
   (D) $4C + 3T + 2B + 16$
   (E) $4C + 3T + 2B + A$

7. Of the following numbers, which is closest to 5.7?

   (A) 5
   (B) 5.5
   (C) 6
   (D) 6.7
   (E) 60

8. Which of the following shapes can be formed using only black, overlapping circles?

   (A)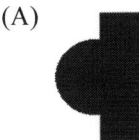

   (B)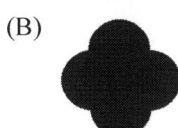

   (C)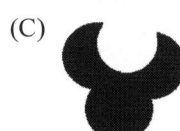

   (D)

   (E)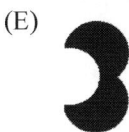

GO ON TO THE NEXT PAGE.

9. If $Q < 2$ and $Q > -1$, which of the following could be a value of Q?

   (A) −3
   (B) −1
   (C) 0
   (D) 2
   (E) 2.5

10. 60 people are seated at a large table, with the same number of people on each side. The table could be any one of the following shapes EXCEPT

    (A) a triangle
    (B) a square
    (C) a pentagon
    (D) a hexagon
    (E) an octagon

11. In a class of 18 students, one sixth have red hair, one sixth have blond hair, and the remainder have brown hair. How many students have brown hair?

    (A) 3
    (B) 6
    (C) 9
    (D) 12
    (E) 15

USE THIS SPACE FOR FIGURING.

GO ON TO THE NEXT PAGE.

USE THIS SPACE FOR FIGURING.

12. Dan is creating a list of songs in the following pattern: one classical song, one rock song, one country song, one jazz song, one blues song. If this pattern continues, the 48th song in his list will be

    (A) classical
    (B) rock
    (C) country
    (D) jazz
    (E) blues

13. If the ratio of 5 : 12 is the same as X : 144, then $X =$

    (A) 10
    (B) 25
    (C) 50
    (D) 55
    (E) 60

14. Which of the following is equal to $4/5$?

    (A) $12/15$
    (B) $16/25$
    (C) $2 \times 2/10$
    (D) $5/4 \times 1/2$
    (E) $4/5 \times 4/5$

15. If $z - 20 = 20$, then $z + 20 =$

    (A) 0
    (B) 20
    (C) 40
    (D) 60
    (E) 80

GO ON TO THE NEXT PAGE.

16. Enrique and 4 other friends evenly split the cost of a cake. If the cake cost x dollars, how much did each person contribute?

    (A) x dollars
    (B) $\dfrac{x}{4}$ dollars
    (C) $4x$ dollars
    (D) $x/5$ dollars
    (E) $x/4 + 1$ dollars

17. Joe bought a bag of candy. He first gave 50% of the bag to his brother, and he then gave 10 pieces of candy to his sister. Afterwards, Joe had 11 pieces of candy left. How many pieces of candy were originally in the bag?

    (A) 10
    (B) 21
    (C) 28
    (D) 42
    (E) 52

18. Figure 2 is made from pieces A and B. If A is a square and B is a trapezoid, what is the perimeter of Figure 2?

    (A) 20
    (B) 26
    (C) 28
    (D) 32
    (E) It cannot be determined from the information given.

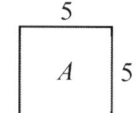
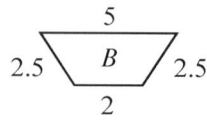
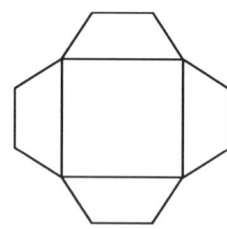

Figure 2

Questions 19 – 20 are based on the graph in Figure 3.

19. In total, how many students in Mr. Khan's class were born in the winter months (December-March)?

    (A) 14
    (B) 16
    (C) 18
    (D) 20
    (E) 21

20. The number of students born in October is what fraction of the number of students born in September?

    (A) $1/12$
    (B) $1/8$
    (C) $1/6$
    (D) $1/4$
    (E) $1/3$

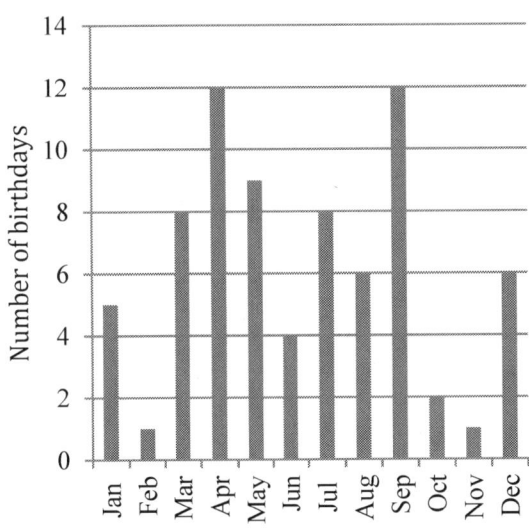

Figure 3

21. If N is a negative number, which of the following expressions has the greatest value?

    (A) $-N/2$
    (B) $N - 2$
    (C) $N - 3$
    (D) N
    (E) $2N$

22. If the area of a square is 1 cm², what is the perimeter of the square?

    (A) 1 cm
    (B) 2 cm
    (C) 3 cm
    (D) 4 cm
    (E) 8 cm

GO ON TO THE NEXT PAGE.

23. Mike's soccer team has won 4 games and lost 7 games. There are 11 more games left in the season. How many more games must Mike's team win in order to have an equal number of wins and losses for the whole season?

    (A) 4
    (B) 7
    (C) 9
    (D) 10
    (E) 11

24. The sum of four consecutive even numbers is 68. What is the smallest number?

    (A) 10
    (B) 12
    (C) 14
    (D) 16
    (E) 18

25. $\dfrac{5^2 - 1}{12} =$

    (A) $1/3$
    (B) $5/12$
    (C) $1/2$
    (D) 1
    (E) 2

STOP

IF YOU FINISH BEFORE TIME IS CALLED,
YOU MAY CHECK YOUR WORK ON THIS SECTION ONLY.
DO NOT TURN TO ANY OTHER SECTION IN THE TEST.

SECTION 2
40 Questions

Read each passage carefully and then answer the questions about it. For each question, decide on the basis of the passage which one of the choices best answers the question.

The sun shines with different degrees of heating power at different parts of the world. Where its effect is greatest, the air is hottest. Now, imagine that at a certain moment the air all around the globe is at one temperature. Then suddenly the sun shines and heats the air at one point until it is much warmer than the surrounding air. The heated air expands, rises, and spreads out above the cold air. But
Line 5   because a certain volume of warm air has less weight than an equal volume of cold air, the cold air starts to rush towards another point and squeeze the rest of the warm air out. You can picture the atmosphere as made up of a number of colder currents passing along the surface of the earth to replace warm currents rising and spreading over the upper surface of the cold air.

1. What is the author's main topic in this passage?

    (A) the temperature of the sun
    (B) the elements that make up air
    (C) how air currents are formed
    (D) how clouds are created
    (E) the size of the earth

2. The author's purpose in this passage is to

    (A) confuse
    (B) entertain
    (C) influence
    (D) educate
    (E) impress

3. According to the passage, cold air currents

    (A) travel lower than hot air currents
    (B) travel higher than hot air currents
    (C) are faster than hot air currents
    (D) are caused by snow
    (E) cause storms

4. What topic would the author most likely discuss next?

    (A) why hot air is less dense than cold air
    (B) the type of weather in different regions of the world
    (C) qualities of the atmospheres on other planets
    (D) the importance of sunlight for plant growth
    (E) other factors affecting air currents on the earth

GO ON TO THE NEXT PAGE.

In an arm-chair, with an elbow resting on the table and her head leaning on that hand, sat the strangest lady I have ever seen, or shall ever see.

She was dressed in rich materials,—satins, and lace, and silks,—all of white. Her shoes were white. She had a long white veil dependent from her hair, and she had bridal flowers in her hair, but her hair was white. Some bright jewels sparkled on her neck and on her hands. Dresses and half-packed trunks were scattered about. Her watch and chain were not put on, and her handkerchief, gloves, some flowers, and a Prayer-Book, were all confusedly heaped about the looking-glass.

I saw that everything within my view which ought to be white, had been white long ago, and had lost its luster and was faded and yellow. I saw that the bride within the bridal dress had withered like the dress, and like the flowers, and had no brightness left but the brightness of her sunken eyes. I saw that the dress had been put upon the rounded figure of a young woman, and that the figure upon which it now hung loose had shrunk to skin and bone. Once, I had been taken to see some ghastly waxwork at the Fair. Once, I had been taken to one of our old marsh churches to see a skeleton in the ashes of a rich dress that had been dug out of a vault under the church pavement. Now, waxwork and skeleton seemed to have dark eyes that moved and looked at me. I should have cried out, if I could.

5. As it is used in line 9, the word "luster" most closely means

(A) money
(B) brightness
(C) softness
(D) dirt
(E) flowers

6. The mood of the room could best be described as

(A) eerie
(B) hospitable
(C) bland
(D) euphoric
(E) oppressive

7. Which of the following is NOT listed as one of the objects in the room?

(A) white gloves
(B) a wedding dress
(C) a book
(D) an old woman
(E) a white bird

8. The author most likely describes the skeleton and waxwork in order to

(A) provide comic relief
(B) distract the reader
(C) tell the reader where the woman came from
(D) build a feeling of suspense and horror
(E) give a history lesson

GO ON TO THE NEXT PAGE.

9. When the author states that "the bride within the bridal dress had withered like the dress" (lines 9-10), he means that

   (A) the woman has grown very old
   (B) the woman is living in squalor
   (C) the woman is shy
   (D) the woman and her dress have been dug out of a vault
   (E) the woman's beauty is immortal

GO ON TO THE NEXT PAGE.

Lack of vitamin A can cause poor vision, including poor night vision, and vision can be restored by adding the vitamin back into the diet. Some people even believe that eating large quantities of carrots will allow one to see in the dark. This misconception developed from stories of British gunners in World War II, who were able to shoot down German planes in the darkness of night thanks to recent advances
Line 5 in radar technology. In an attempt to cover up their effective use of radar in engaging enemy planes, the British Air Force circulated a rumor that eating carrots enabled their pilots to see German planes in the dark. This propaganda reinforced existing German fears, and it helped encourage carrot consumption among Britons looking to improve their night vision during blackouts.

10. It can be inferred from the passage that

    (A) vegetables have no effect on vision
    (B) eating meat will hurt your ability to see in the dark
    (C) carrots are a source of vitamin A
    (D) carrots are the healthiest vegetable
    (E) animals that have good night vision eat a lot of carrots

11. According to the passage, what role did the British Air Force play in the belief that carrots can provide the ability to see in the dark?

    (A) British Air Force scientists discovered this property of carrots during World War II.
    (B) The British Air Force intentionally spread this rumor to misinform the Germans.
    (C) The British Air Force tried to stop this rumor from reaching the Germans.
    (D) The British Air Force told this rumor to their pilots in order to justify the carrots in their rations.
    (E) When the British Air Force heard this rumor, they encouraged their pilots to eat carrots.

12. According to the passage, the British gunners were actually able to shoot down German planes at night because

    (A) the British ate carrots to improve their night vision
    (B) the light emitted by the German planes made them easy to see
    (C) the British had naturally better eyesight than the Germans
    (D) the British outnumbered the Germans
    (E) the British used radar technologies to find the planes

13. Which of the following would be a good title for this passage?

    (A) The Discovery of Vitamin A
    (B) Carrots and Night Vision: Fact and Fiction
    (C) British Air Tactics in World War II
    (D) How to Grow Carrots
    (E) The Use of Propaganda in Great Britain

GO ON TO THE NEXT PAGE.

Line 5

Montgomery, Alabama, is located in a beautiful spot on the Alabama River, near the center of the state. Its position at the head of navigation on the Alabama river, its connection by railway with important points, and the rich agricultural country with which it is surrounded make it a great commercial center and the second largest city in the state in terms of wealth and population. It is the capital, and consequently attracts many learned men and great politicians, giving it a society of the highest rank and making it the social center of the state.

From 1858 to 1860, the South enjoyed great prosperity. "Cotton was king," and millions of dollars were poured into the country to purchase it. A fair share of that money found its way to Montgomery.

10

When planters from the surrounding towns had gathered their crops (as well as tobacco and rice), they sent them away to the city of Montgomery to be sold and deposited the proceeds in its banks. During their busy season, they had hardly any social contact outside their own families. However, when their crops were gathered, they left their plantations and went with their families, where they gave themselves up to enjoyment, spending their money in a most lavish manner.

14. The primary topic of this passage is

(A) how cotton is grown
(B) plantations in Alabama
(C) the origins of Southern society
(D) slavery in Montgomery
(E) Montgomery's history of prosperity

15. The author claims that Montgomery

I. has the largest population of any city in Alabama
II. is the social center of Alabama
III. was the site of large cotton plantations

(A) I only
(B) I and II only
(C) II only
(D) II and III only
(E) I, II and III

16. According to the passage, Montgomery was prosperous for all of the following reasons EXCEPT

(A) access to transportation, such as rivers and railways
(B) good agricultural land
(C) wealthy planters
(D) gold mines
(E) tobacco production

17. When the author states that "Cotton was king" (line 7), he likely means that

(A) cotton was a very important crop
(B) the king of Montgomery was named Cotton
(C) farmers were only allowed to grow cotton
(D) Montgomery was the only place that grew cotton
(E) the mayor of Montgomery was required by law to be a farmer

GO ON TO THE NEXT PAGE.

18. According to the passage, Alabama planters went to Montgomery mainly to

    (A) get away from their families
    (B) gather their crops
    (C) educate their children and families
    (D) enjoy themselves after their busy season was over
    (E) purchase cotton

19. The author of the passage would most likely agree that

    (A) Alabama planters should not have spent so much money on entertainment
    (B) Alabama planters were important in making Montgomery a great city
    (C) no Northern city can compare to Montgomery
    (D) learned men and women are more likely to be found in a university town than in a state capital
    (E) the cotton trade was immoral

GO ON TO THE NEXT PAGE.

> Line 5
> It is not the critic who counts; not the man who points out how the strong man stumbles, or where the doer of deeds could have done them better. The credit belongs to the man who is actually in the arena, whose face is marred by dust and sweat and blood; who strives valiantly; who errs, who comes short again and again, because there is no effort without error and shortcoming; but who does actually strive to do the deeds; who knows great enthusiasms, the great devotions; who spends himself in a worthy cause; who at the best knows in the end the triumph of high achievement, and who at the worst, if he fails, at least fails while daring greatly, so that his place shall never be with those cold and timid souls who neither know victory nor defeat.

20. Which of the following best expresses the main idea of this passage?

    (A) It is better to try and risk failure than never to try at all.
    (B) One should only attempt to do something if one is sure of success.
    (C) Criticism doesn't help anyone.
    (D) Critics are the most productive members of society.
    (E) It is necessary to have many friends in order to attempt great tasks.

21. The author's tone in this passage could best be described as

    (A) sarcastic
    (B) cautious
    (C) melancholy
    (D) disinterested
    (E) emphatic

22. The author suggests that a man who attempts great things is like

    (A) a critic
    (B) a competitor in an arena
    (C) a general leading an army
    (D) a businessman
    (E) a mountain-climber

23. What is the author's primary purpose in this passage?

    (A) to celebrate athletes
    (B) to support strategic thinking
    (C) to warn of the dangers of failure
    (D) to praise risk-takers
    (E) to encourage skepticism

24. The speaker would most likely NOT admire someone who

    (A) tries to scale a dangerous mountain, but dies along the way
    (B) hunts down a notorious criminal, but never finds him
    (C) campaigns for office with enthusiasm and integrity, but loses
    (D) complains about the food in a restaurant, but has never tried to cook a meal
    (E) runs a marathon, but comes in last place

GO ON TO THE NEXT PAGE.

> Love is like the wild rose-briar;
> Friendship like the holly-tree.
> The holly is dark when the rose-briar blooms,
> But which will bloom most constantly?
> *Line 5* The wild rose-briar is sweet in spring,
> Its summer blossoms scent the air;
> Yet wait till winter comes again,
> And who will call the wild-briar fair?
> Then, scorn the silly rose-wreath now,
> *10* And deck thee with the holly's sheen,
> That, when December blights thy brow,
> He still may leave thy garland green.

25. Which of the following would be the best title for this passage?

    (A) The Fickle Friend
    (B) Cruel December
    (C) Love and Friendship
    (D) The Seasons
    (E) A Rose for Remembrance

26. Which of the following best expresses the main idea of this poem?

    (A) Keep your friends close and your enemies closer.
    (B) When decorating with plants, choose long-lasting ones.
    (C) Roses are not as beautiful as holly.
    (D) Love always ends poorly.
    (E) Friendship is more long-lasting than love.

27. The speaker implies that in the winter, the rose-briar

    (A) continues to bloom beautifully
    (B) grows sharp thorns
    (C) loses its beautiful, scented blossoms
    (D) is green and shiny
    (E) can be used to make bouquets, but not wreaths

28. The poem suggests that just as holly remains fresh and green throughout the winter, friendship

    (A) can become bitter during the winter
    (B) can withstand the tests of time
    (C) grows stale and tired
    (D) is more fun during the holidays
    (E) is never as fulfilling as love

29. What does the author mean when she advises the reader to "scorn the silly rose-wreath now, and deck thee with the holly's sheen" (lines 9-10)?

    (A) Place importance in friendship rather than love.
    (B) Tell your loved ones what you think of them now, before they get old.
    (C) Throw away any roses in your house.
    (D) Invite people over for a holiday party.
    (E) Protect yourself from people who want to take advantage from you.

GO ON TO THE NEXT PAGE.

During the "Golden Age" of Hollywood—from the early 1920s through the early 1950s—Hollywood movies were produced and distributed through what is known as the studio system. The term refers to two important practices of large motion picture studios at the time: they produced movies primarily on their own filmmaking lots with creative personnel under long-term contracts; and they owned, or effectively controlled, the movie theaters to which they distributed their films. These two practices helped the top studios maximize their profits and maintain control of the industry.

Studios controlled almost completely what jobs the actors under contract with them could or could not do, which was understandably frustrating for some performers. In the late 1930s, Cary Grant became the first Hollywood star to "go independent" by not renewing his studio contract. By leaving the studio system, Grant gained control over every aspect of his career, although he also ran the risk of that career dwindling because no particular studio had a long-term interest in promoting it. For Grant, the risk paid off. Not only able to decide which films he was going to appear in, he often had personal choice of his directors and co-stars. At times he even negotiated a share of the gross revenue, something uncommon at the time. Grant received more than $700,000 for his 10% of the gross profits for *To Catch a Thief*, while Alfred Hitchcock received less than $50,000 for directing and producing it.

30. Which of the following would be the best title for this passage?

   (A) Cary Grant Catches $700,000 for *To Catch a Thief*
   (B) The Greed of Motion Picture Studios
   (C) The Birth of Hollywood
   (D) Cary Grant and the Studio System
   (E) How to be a Star

31. According to the passage, which of the following factors contributed to the strength of the major motion picture studios in the 1920s – 1950s?

   I. the studios' long-term contracts with actors
   II. the studios' ownership of the lots where they made their films
   III. independent stars like Cary Grant

   (A) I only
   (B) II only
   (C) III only
   (D) I and II only
   (E) I, II, and III

GO ON TO THE NEXT PAGE.

32. According to the passage, Cary Grant and other actors decided to "go independent" (line 9) because

    (A) they wanted to own movie theaters and filmmaking lots
    (B) they wanted to maximize their profits
    (C) they wanted control over what jobs they could do
    (D) they wanted to work with Alfred Hitchcock
    (E) they wanted to direct and produce their own films

33. According to the passage, when Cary Grant left the studio system, he ran the risk of

    (A) choosing bad roles to play in future films
    (B) losing the favor of his audiences, who were loyal to the studio system
    (C) bankrupting the motion picture industry
    (D) his career suffering without the support of a studio
    (E) losing control over his career

34. Which of the following questions is NOT answered by information in the passage?

    (A) Who was the first Hollywood star to leave the studio system?
    (B) What were the components of the studio system?
    (C) About how much money was made by the movie *To Catch a Thief*?
    (D) When was the "Golden Age" of Hollywood?
    (E) Who was Cary Grant's favorite director?

35. The author of the passage would most likely agree that

    (A) many actors want to be able to choose their roles
    (B) Cary Grant was Hollywood's most talented actor
    (C) the Supreme Court overstepped its bounds by ruling against the studio system
    (D) Hollywood movies in the 1920s were not very good
    (E) actors today have too much power

GO ON TO THE NEXT PAGE.

One June evening, when the orchards were pink blossomed again, when the frogs were singing silverly sweet in the marshes about the head of the Lake of Shining Waters, and the air was full of the savor of clover fields and balsamic fir woods, Anne had fallen into wide-eyed reverie, looking out past the boughs of the Snow Queen, once more bestarred with its tufts of blossom.

Line 5
    In all essential respects the little gable chamber was unchanged. The walls were as white, the pincushion as hard, the chairs as stiffly and yellowly upright as ever. Yet the whole character of the room was altered. Anne thought that it was full of a new vital, pulsing personality that seemed to pervade it. It was as if all the dreams, sleeping and waking, of its vivid occupant had taken a visible although unmaterial form and had tapestried the bare room with splendid filmy tissues of rainbow and moonshine.

36. Which of the following best describes the mood of this scene?

(A) suspenseful
(B) gloomy
(C) mystical
(D) cynical
(E) uproarious

37. Which of the following images, if added to the passage, would best fit with the author's description of the June evening in the first sentence?

(A) the honking of cars and buses
(B) a cold, gray fog
(C) shopkeepers busily closing their stores
(D) the smell of pizza in the oven
(E) the golden glow of the setting sun

38. In the context of the passage, the "Snow Queen" described in line 4 most likely refers to

(A) a tree
(B) an imaginary friend
(C) a sorceress
(D) a hill
(E) a dog

39. When the author states that "the whole character of the room was altered" (lines 6-7), she means that

(A) Anne had decorated the room with brightly colored cloth
(B) the room appeared different to Anne because of her dreams
(C) the Snow Queen had enchanted the room
(D) a prism in the window was casting rainbows on the walls
(E) the room had been newly painted white

GO ON TO THE NEXT PAGE.

40. Based on the passage, Anne can be best described as

    (A) realistic
    (B) imaginative
    (C) fearful
    (D) domineering
    (E) immature

STOP
IF YOU FINISH BEFORE TIME IS CALLED,
YOU MAY CHECK YOUR WORK ON THIS SECTION ONLY.
DO NOT TURN TO ANY OTHER SECTION IN THE TEST.

SECTION 3
60 Questions

This section consists of two different types of questions: synonyms and analogies. There are directions and a sample question for each type.

Synonyms

Each of the following questions consists of one word followed by five words or phrases. You are to select the one word or phrase whose meaning is closest to the word in capital letters.

Sample Question:

CHILLY:

(A) lazy
(B) nice
(C) dry
(D) cold
(E) sunny

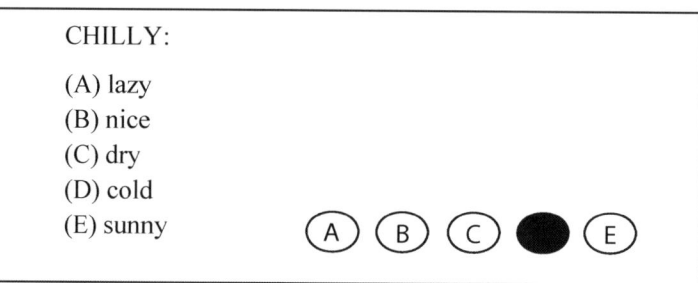

---

1. RIGID:
   (A) not flexible
   (B) thorough
   (C) not direct
   (D) cold
   (E) sympathetic

2. REFLEX:
   (A) muscular strength
   (B) new abilities
   (C) traditional garb
   (D) food sample
   (E) instinctive reaction

3. DENY:
   (A) stream
   (B) refuse
   (C) lie
   (D) encourage
   (E) respond

4. MOPE:
   (A) polish
   (B) sleep
   (C) pace
   (D) smile
   (E) pout

5. EAGER:
   (A) thoughtful
   (B) bored
   (C) inspired
   (D) overjoyed
   (E) enthusiastic

6. SIMPLE:
   (A) boring
   (B) silent
   (C) nice
   (D) plain
   (E) pretty

GO ON TO THE NEXT PAGE.

7. QUAKE:
   - (A) shake
   - (B) stake
   - (C) fall
   - (D) slam
   - (E) laugh

8. SIGNAL:
   - (A) acknowledge
   - (B) obscure
   - (C) indicate
   - (D) assail
   - (E) assume

9. AUTHORIZE:
   - (A) demand
   - (B) refill
   - (C) attempt
   - (D) permit
   - (E) decorate

10. LEGISLATE:
    - (A) take control
    - (B) make into law
    - (C) select leaders
    - (D) read aloud
    - (E) vote for

11. YIELD:
    - (A) surrender
    - (B) imply
    - (C) avoid
    - (D) announce
    - (E) reduce

12. PROCLAIM:
    - (A) dance
    - (B) announce
    - (C) protect
    - (D) cheer up
    - (E) insult

13. EXCLUDE:
    - (A) prop up
    - (B) destroy
    - (C) keep out
    - (D) tease
    - (E) slander

14. TRUCE:
    - (A) pine
    - (B) tractor
    - (C) declaration
    - (D) trick
    - (E) cease-fire

15. DEBRIS:
    - (A) exposure
    - (B) rubble
    - (C) fighters
    - (D) surplus
    - (E) platform

16. PROBABLE:
    - (A) likely
    - (B) refutable
    - (C) distinct
    - (D) detestable
    - (E) soft

GO ON TO THE NEXT PAGE.

17. SEVERITY:
    - (A) drought
    - (B) division
    - (C) wound
    - (D) lie
    - (E) harshness

18. LISTLESS:
    - (A) garbled
    - (B) asleep
    - (C) tireless
    - (D) spread out
    - (E) without energy

19. SAGE:
    - (A) spicy
    - (B) wise
    - (C) mossy
    - (D) false
    - (E) cold

20. RESTRAINT:
    - (A) pressure
    - (B) repetition
    - (C) exhaustion
    - (D) reserve
    - (E) rescue

21. WARBLE:
    - (A) trip
    - (B) worry
    - (C) sing
    - (D) assail
    - (E) fall

22. RECOIL:
    - (A) escape
    - (B) braid
    - (C) withdraw
    - (D) unbind
    - (E) slither

23. ENVELOP:
    - (A) entrust
    - (B) cut off
    - (C) freeze
    - (D) enclose
    - (E) inside

24. CREED:
    - (A) avarice
    - (B) belief
    - (C) guilt
    - (D) admiration
    - (E) creation

25. VARIABLE:
    - (A) changeable
    - (B) vertical
    - (C) capable
    - (D) colorful
    - (E) possible

26. ANNUL:
    - (A) cancel
    - (B) record
    - (C) celebrate
    - (D) subtract
    - (E) conceal

GO ON TO THE NEXT PAGE.

27. SURLY:

    (A) bad-tempered
    (B) sweet
    (C) robust
    (D) untidy
    (E) lazy

28. MERCILESS:

    (A) passionate
    (B) insecure
    (C) aggressive
    (D) cynical
    (E) ruthless

29. PUNGENT:

    (A) unlikely
    (B) peripheral
    (C) wet
    (D) smelly
    (E) wicked

30. HUBRIS:

    (A) optimism
    (B) shame
    (C) arrogance
    (D) indifference
    (E) laziness

GO ON TO THE NEXT PAGE.

Analogies

The following questions ask you to find relationships between words. For each question, select the answer choice that best completes the meaning of the sentence.

Sample Question:

> Kitten is to cat as
> (A) fawn is to colt
> (B) puppy is to dog
> (C) cow is to bull
> (D) wolf is to bear
> (E) hen is to rooster

Choice (B) is the best answer because a kitten is a young cat just as a puppy is a young dog. Of all the answer choices, (B) states a relationship that is most like the relationship between kitten and cat.

---

31. Canary is to yellow as
    (A) crow is to purple
    (B) sparrow is to hungry
    (C) robin's egg is to blue
    (D) tiger is to stripes
    (E) green is to envy

32. Principal is to teacher as
    (A) editor is to author
    (B) doctor is to patient
    (C) athlete is to trainer
    (D) manager is to cashier
    (E) lawyer is to client

33. Actor is to monologue as
    (A) animal is to monotone
    (B) script is to improvisation
    (C) play is to theater
    (D) dancer is to solo
    (E) director is to rehearsal

34. Breed is to dog as
    (A) thoroughbred is to horse
    (B) flavor is to ice cream
    (C) feline is to tiger
    (D) ewe is to sheep
    (E) gaggle is to goose

35. Bean is to sprout as
    (A) sapling is to sequoia
    (B) petal is to pedal
    (C) root is to leaf
    (D) bulb is to shoot
    (E) cap is to mushroom

36. Stethoscope is to doctor as
    (A) bat is to pitcher
    (B) gavel is to judge
    (C) scrubs are to nurse
    (D) gyroscope is to electrician
    (E) telescope is to astronomer

GO ON TO THE NEXT PAGE.

37. Relish is to pickles as

   (A) honey is to bees
   (B) mustard is to hotdog
   (C) salsa is to tomatoes
   (D) jam is to jar
   (E) mash is to potatoes

38. Lion is to horse as

   (A) bear is to wolf
   (B) claw is to hoof
   (C) yellow is to brown
   (D) zoo is to circus
   (E) king is to villager

39. Roe is to salmon as

   (A) foe is to haddock
   (B) scale is to boat
   (C) bill is to duck
   (D) bark is to tree
   (E) egg is to chicken

40. Break is to promise as rescind is to

   (A) friendship
   (B) adventure
   (C) qualification
   (D) offer
   (E) symbol

41. Exile is to country as

   (A) expel is to school
   (B) voyage is to land
   (C) incarcerate is to prison
   (D) restrain is to court
   (E) reject is to club

42. Rabbit is to hutch as

   (A) pig is to sty
   (B) wolf is to pack
   (C) caterpillar is to cocoon
   (D) cow is to farm
   (E) gerbil is to wheel

43. Area is to volume as

   (A) depth is to prism
   (B) square is to rectangle
   (C) triangle is to pyramid
   (D) arc is to circle
   (E) line is to segment

44. Bowler is to hat as

   (A) potter is to shoe
   (B) tennis is to beret
   (C) soup is to head
   (D) fowl is to rat
   (E) braid is to hairdo

45. Series is to episode as

   (A) comic book is to cartoon
   (B) tournament is to game
   (C) television is to movies
   (D) incident is to fall
   (E) refrain is to song

46. Emissary is to message as

   (A) paperboy is to newspaper
   (B) statistician is to numbers
   (C) prophet is to danger
   (D) contender is to argument
   (E) pioneer is to invention

GO ON TO THE NEXT PAGE.

47. Flight attendant is to plane as

    (A) captain is to ship
    (B) passenger is to taxi
    (C) waiter is to restaurant
    (D) hydrogen is to blimp
    (E) cashier is to register

48. Twins are to triplets as

    (A) siblings are to cousins
    (B) singles are to couples
    (C) duets are to trios
    (D) twenties are to fifties
    (E) mirrors are to kaleidoscopes

49. Thorn is to rose as

    (A) knot is to wood
    (B) quill is to porcupine
    (C) wart is to toad
    (D) shell is to snail
    (E) needle is to spindle

50. Banana is to peel as

    (A) corn is to kernel
    (B) peach is to skin
    (C) pod is to peas
    (D) apple is to orange
    (E) lemon is to wedge

51. Catastrophe is to problem as

    (A) illness is to symptom
    (B) bliss is to pleasure
    (C) embarrassment is to shame
    (D) ebullience is to euphoria
    (E) illumination is to light

52. Reclusive is to sociable as

    (A) hermetic is to happy
    (B) quiet is to nice
    (C) friendly is to likeable
    (D) angry is to impressive
    (E) taciturn is to chatty

53. Period is to sentence as

    (A) checkmate is to chess game
    (B) curtain is to play
    (C) arrest is to case
    (D) yoyo is to string
    (E) crying is to movie

54. Aimless is to direction as reckless is to

    (A) speed
    (B) energy
    (C) anger
    (D) hope
    (E) caution

55. Planet is to solar system as

    (A) horse is to carousel
    (B) duck is to pond
    (C) leaves are to tree
    (D) students are to school
    (E) molecule is to atom

56. Brush is to painter as

    (A) paper is to draftsman
    (B) essay is to academic
    (C) bow is to violinist
    (D) shoes are to dancer
    (E) clay is to sculpture

GO ON TO THE NEXT PAGE.

57. Zesty is to flavor as

   (A) zero is to favor
   (B) zippy is to energy
   (C) zebra is to fur
   (D) zodiac is to ecology
   (E) zap is to fire

58. Root is to tree as

   (A) switch is to appliance
   (B) petal is to flower
   (C) branch is to canopy
   (D) leg is to arm
   (E) foundation is to building

59. Silk is to wool as

   (A) taffeta is to gingham
   (B) plaid is to paisley
   (C) orange is to red
   (D) silkworm is to sheep
   (E) sun is to snow

60. Violet is to vanilla as

   (A) fuchsia is to red
   (B) tangy is to mint
   (C) sound is to smell
   (D) rose is to cinnamon
   (E) blue is to color

STOP

IF YOU FINISH BEFORE TIME IS CALLED,
YOU MAY CHECK YOUR WORK ON THIS SECTION ONLY.
DO NOT TURN TO ANY OTHER SECTION IN THE TEST.

SECTION 4
25 Questions

Following each problem in this section, there are five suggested answers. Work out each problem in your head or in the blank space provided at the right of the page. Then look at the five suggested answers and decide which one is best.

Note: Figures that accompany problems in this section are drawn as accurately as possible EXCEPT when it is stated in a specific problem that its figure is not drawn to scale.

Sample problem:

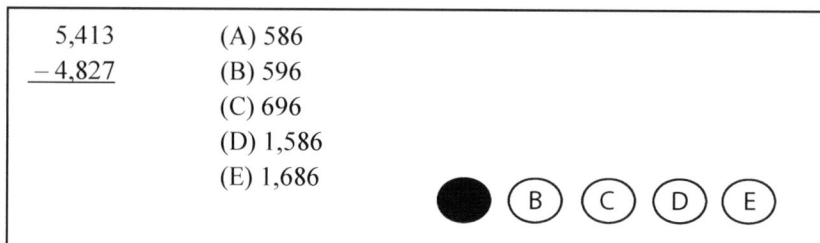

USE THIS SPACE FOR FIGURING.

1. What is the next number in the pattern below?

    2, 4, 6, 10, 16, 26, ___

    (A) 28
    (B) 30
    (C) 34
    (D) 42
    (E) 60

2. There are three dozen cookies. If five children each eat four cookies, how many cookies are left?

    (A) 0
    (B) 12
    (C) 16
    (D) 20
    (E) 31

GO ON TO THE NEXT PAGE.

3. A taxi charges A dollars for the first mile and B cents for each additional mile. How much would a 5-mile ride cost, in cents?

   (A) $A + 5B$
   (B) $A + 4B$
   (C) $5A + 5B$
   (D) $100A + 4B$
   (E) $100A + 5B$

4. Which of the following shapes CANNOT be drawn without lifting the pencil or retracing?

   (A) [circle with cross inside]
   (B) [six-pointed star overlapping rectangle]
   (C) [curved figure-eight-like shape]
   (D) [three connected hexagons]
   (E) [arrow with curved tail]

5. If P is an even number, which of the following must also be an even number?

   (A) $P + 1$
   (B) $P + 3$
   (C) $2P + 1$
   (D) $3P$
   (E) $3P + 1$

GO ON TO THE NEXT PAGE.

Practice Test 1: Middle Level

USE THIS SPACE FOR FIGURING.

6. Dennis has $7.25, and pencils cost $0.50 each. What is the greatest number of pencils Dennis can buy?

    (A) 7
    (B) 8
    (C) 10
    (D) 12
    (E) 14

---

7. Kelly brought 100 donuts to a club meeting. By the end of the meeting, 50 donuts were eaten. What percentage of donuts were uneaten?

    (A) $\frac{1}{2}$%
    (B) 5%
    (C) 25%
    (D) 50%
    (E) 60%

---

8. It takes Michael 1 minute and 30 seconds to run a lap. At that rate, how many laps can Michael run in 15 minutes?

    (A) 5
    (B) 10
    (C) 15
    (D) 20
    (E) 30

GO ON TO THE NEXT PAGE.

Questions 9 – 11 refer to the graph in Figure 1.

9. Which of the following statements is correct?

    (A) Last year, Hailey had the most toys
    (B) Last year, Aidan had the fewest toys
    (C) This year, Kayla has 10 more toys than Hailey
    (D) This year, Aidan has exactly 5 more toys than he did last year
    (E) This year, Kayla has twice as many toys as she did last year

10. About how many toys did Hailey, Aidan, and Kayla have in total last year?

    (A) 35
    (B) 40
    (C) 44
    (D) 50
    (E) 52

11. This year, Hailey, Aiden, and Kayla have an average of how many toys each?

    (A) 15
    (B) 20
    (C) 22.5
    (D) 25
    (E) 27.5

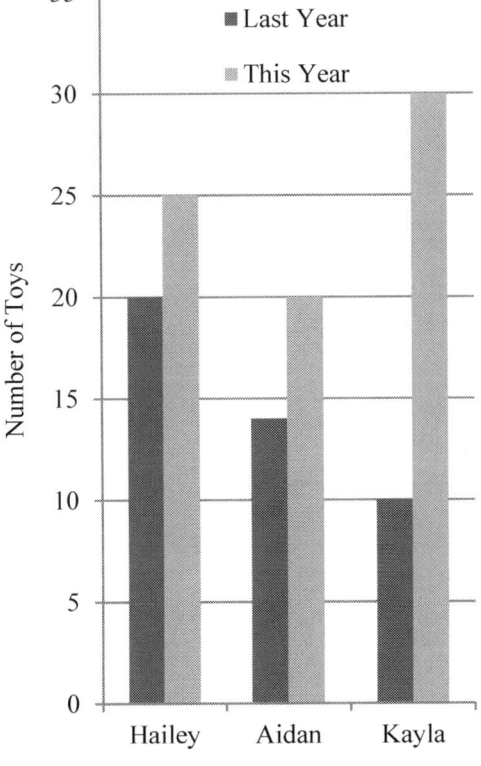

Figure 1

12. Which of the following is closest to 0.32 × 59?

    (A) $1/6$ of 50
    (B) $1/6$ of 60
    (C) $1/3$ of 50
    (D) $1/2$ of 50
    (E) $1/3$ of 60

13. Figure 2 shows two squares, one with a side length of 4 and one with a side length of 7. The perimeter of the entire figure is

    (A) 16
    (B) 20
    (C) 33
    (D) 36
    (E) 44

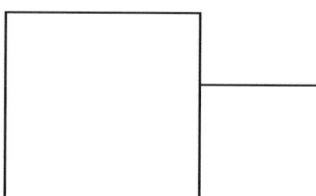
Figure 2

14. $7 \times 1/7$ is equal to

    (A) $1/7$
    (B) $2/7$
    (C) 1
    (D) 7
    (E) 49

15. If Karim has fifteen pails and 60% of them are full, how many are NOT full?

    (A) 4
    (B) 6
    (C) 7
    (D) 8
    (E) 9

GO ON TO THE NEXT PAGE.

16. In Figure 3, four line segments are drawn from the midpoints of a large square to make a smaller shaded square. If the area of the large square is z, then the area of the shaded square is

    (A) z
    (B) $\frac{1}{2}z$
    (C) $\frac{1}{3}z$
    (D) $\frac{1}{4}z$
    (E) $\frac{1}{5}z$

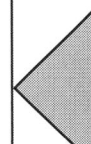

Figure 3

17. If $2Y + 30$ is less than 36, what could be a possible value of Y?

    (A) 0
    (B) 3
    (C) 4
    (D) 5
    (E) 10

18. In Figure 4, what is the value of x?

    (A) 35
    (B) 45
    (C) 55
    (D) 65
    (E) 75

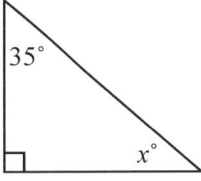

Figure 4

19. If Q is a positive number, which of the following expressions has the smallest value?

    (A) $2 + Q$
    (B) $-4 - Q$
    (C) $Q - 2$
    (D) $(-Q)^2$
    (E) $-Q$

20. Melanie usually drives to work with 5 other people, and they all share the cost of gas evenly. Today, only 3 other people are driving with Melanie. If they still share the cost of gas evenly, which of the following must be true?

(A) Each person will need to contribute more for gas.

(B) Each person will need to contribute less for gas.

(C) Some people will contribute more for gas than others.

(D) The amount each person contributes for gas will stay the same.

(E) None of the above.

21. A teacher is arranging a large group of students into a line with the following pattern: boy, girl, boy, boy, girl, girl, boy, girl, boy, boy, girl, girl... If the same pattern continues, what will be the gender of the 54th and 55th student in the line?

(A) boy, boy

(B) girl, girl

(C) girl, boy

(D) boy, girl

(E) It cannot be determined from the information given.

22. Which of the following is greater than $3/5$?

(A) $1/2$

(B) $22/36$

(C) $21/35$

(D) $11/20$

(E) $3/9$

USE THIS SPACE FOR FIGURING.

23. If ★$x = (x + 2) + 1$, then ★$5 =$

    (A) 8
    (B) 11
    (C) 15
    (D) 16
    (E) 50

24. 40% of 80 is equal to y. What multiplied by y is equal to 16?

    (A) $\frac{1}{2}$
    (B) $\frac{1}{4}$
    (C) 1
    (D) 2
    (E) 3

25. What is the product of the first five positive integers?

    (A) 0
    (B) 15
    (C) 24
    (D) 100
    (E) 120

STOP

IF YOU FINISH BEFORE TIME IS CALLED,
YOU MAY CHECK YOUR WORK ON THIS SECTION ONLY.
DO NOT TURN TO ANY OTHER SECTION IN THE TEST.

Middle Level
Practice Test 2

How to Take this Practice Test

To simulate an accurate testing environment, sit at a desk in a quiet location free of distractions—no TV, computers, phones, music, or noise—and clear your desk of all materials except pencils and erasers. Remember that no calculators, rulers, protractors, dictionaries, or other aids are allowed on the SSAT.

Give yourself the following amounts of time for each section:

Section	Subject	Time Limit
	Writing	25 minutes
	5-minute break	
1	Math I	30 minutes
2	Reading	40 minutes
	5-minute break	
3	Verbal	30 minutes
4	Math II	30 minutes

Have an adult help you monitor your time, or use a stopwatch and time yourself. Only give yourself the allotted time for each section; put your pencil down when your time is up. Note: timing may be extended for students with diagnosed learning disabilities who apply for testing with accommodations.

Follow the instructions carefully. As you take your test, bubble your answers into the answer sheets provided. Use the test booklet as scratch paper for notes and calculations. Remember that you are not granted time at the end of a section to transfer your answers to the answer sheet, so you must do this as you go along.

When you are finished, check your answers against the answer keys provided. Then, score your exam using the directions at the end.

Be sure each mark completely fills the answer space.
Start with number 1 for each new section of the test. You may find more answer spaces than you need. If so, please leave them blank.

SECTION 1

(blank answer grid, questions 1–25, options A B C D E)

SECTION 2

(blank answer grid, questions 1–40, options A B C D E)

SECTION 3

(blank answer grid, questions 1–60, options A B C D E)

SECTION 4

(blank answer grid, questions 1–25, options A B C D E)

Practice Test 2: Middle Level

Writing Sample

Schools would like to get to know you better through a story you tell using one of the ideas below. Please choose the idea you find most interesting and write a story using the idea as your first sentence. Please fill in the circle next to the one you choose.

(A) I turned the corner and ...

(B) They said it did not exist.

Use this page and the next page to complete your writing sample.

Continue on next page

SECTION 1
25 Questions

Following each problem in this section, there are five suggested answers. Work out each problem in your head or in the blank space provided at the right of the page. Then look at the five suggested answers and decide which one is best.

Note: Figures that accompany problems in this section are drawn as accurately as possible EXCEPT when it is stated in a specific problem that its figure is not drawn to scale.

Sample problem:

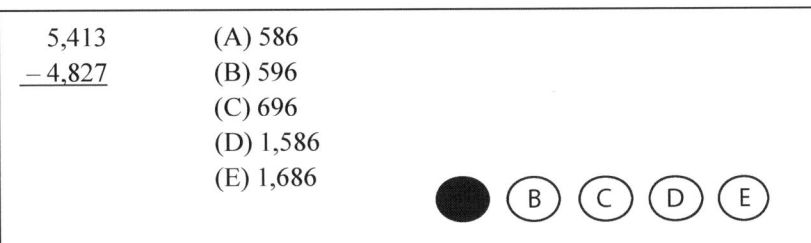

USE THIS SPACE FOR FIGURING.

1. If $3x = 39$, then $x =$

    (A) 10
    (B) 11
    (C) 12
    (D) 13
    (E) 39

2. If 50% of a number is 40, what is the number?

    (A) 20
    (B) 40
    (C) 60
    (D) 80
    (E) 100

GO ON TO THE NEXT PAGE.

Practice Test 2: Middle Level

USE THIS SPACE FOR FIGURING.

3. Robert needs 26 rolls of tape. If there are 4 rolls of tape in a package, how many packages does Robert need to buy?

   (A) 3
   (B) 4
   (C) 5
   (D) 6
   (E) 7

4. $\frac{3}{8} + 4\frac{10}{16} =$

   (A) 4
   (B) $4\frac{8}{16}$
   (C) $4\frac{13}{24}$
   (D) $4\frac{13}{16}$
   (E) 5

5. If $3N + 2 = 20$, then $N =$

   (A) 0
   (B) 6
   (C) 7
   (D) 10
   (E) 15

6. If $M \times P = 17$, which of the following CANNOT be the value of P?

   (A) 0
   (B) $1/17$
   (C) 1
   (D) 17
   (E) 34

GO ON TO THE NEXT PAGE.

USE THIS SPACE FOR FIGURING.

7. Deborah is on floor *F* in the department store. If she goes up 3 floors and takes the elevator down 7 floors, she reaches the second floor. What floor is floor *F*?

   (A) the 4th floor
   (B) the 5th floor
   (C) the 6th floor
   (D) the 8th floor
   (E) the 12th floor

8. What is the next number in the sequence below?

   0.10, 0.21, 0.32, 0.43, ____

   (A) 0.43
   (B) 0.44
   (C) 0.45
   (D) 0.54
   (E) 0.55

9. McKayla is selecting a box to hold 750 cubic centimeters of juice. Which of the following dimensions will be the best fit?

   (A) 6 mm × 5 mm × 25 mm
   (B) 5 mm × 10 mm × 15 mm
   (C) 5 cm × 5 mm × 25 cm
   (D) 5 cm × 10 cm × 15 cm
   (E) 6 cm × 5 cm × 20 cm

10. If a number is greater than 3, then 3 times that number must be greater than

    (A) $1/3$
    (B) 1
    (C) 3
    (D) 6
    (E) 9

GO ON TO THE NEXT PAGE.

Practice Test 2: Middle Level

11. What is the remainder when 109 is divided by 37?

    (A) 2
    (B) 18
    (C) 22
    (D) 35
    (E) 72

12. The length of a rectangle is two times its width. If the width of the rectangle is 3 meters, what is the perimeter of the rectangle?

    (A) 6 meters
    (B) 9 meters
    (C) 18 meters
    (D) 36 meters
    (E) 72 meters

13. Lindsay has two sons and one daughter. Each of Lindsay's sons has two children, and her daughter has three children. How many grandchildren does Lindsay have?

    (A) 3
    (B) 4
    (C) 6
    (D) 7
    (E) 10

USE THIS SPACE FOR FIGURING.

GO ON TO THE NEXT PAGE.

14. A group of 3 knitters takes 3 hours to knit a total of 6 sweaters. Sally can knit 6 sweaters in 3 hours working by herself. If Sally joins the group of knitters, what will be the new average rate for each knitter?

   (A) $1/2$ sweaters per hour
   (B) $2/3$ sweaters per hour
   (C) 1 sweater per hour
   (D) $4/3$ sweaters per hour
   (E) It cannot be determined from the information given.

---

15. Rocky selects a point on the grid in Figure 1. He then moves three units left, one unit up, one unit right, and five units down. If he ends up at point P, what was his starting point?

    (A) F
    (B) G
    (C) H
    (D) J
    (E) K

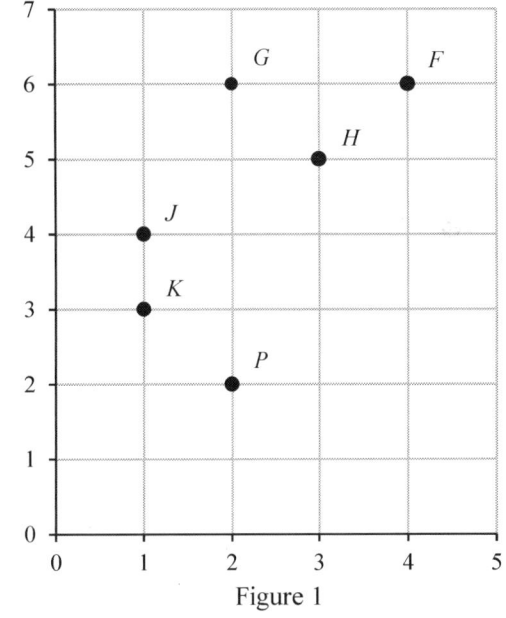

Figure 1

---

16. There are 230 foxes in a forest. If the ratio of rabbits to foxes in the forest is 5 : 2, how many rabbits are in the forest?

    (A) 460
    (B) 575
    (C) 580
    (D) 720
    (E) 1150

GO ON TO THE NEXT PAGE.

17. Juan folds a sheet of paper in half. He then uses scissors to cut out a shape by cutting through both layers of the folded paper. When he unfolds the shape, it could look like any of the following EXCEPT:

(A)

(B)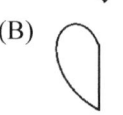

(C)

(D)

(E)

18. If $(5 - W) \times 2 = 6$, then $W =$

(A) 1
(B) 2
(C) 3
(D) 4
(E) 12

19. Jae ran four times this week. She completed her run in 6.5 minutes on Monday, 7.25 minutes on Wednesday, 6 minutes on Friday, and 6.25 minutes on Sunday. What was Jae's average time for each run?

(A) 6.125 min.
(B) 6.5 min.
(C) 6.75 min.
(D) 7 min.
(E) 7.25 min.

GO ON TO THE NEXT PAGE.

Questions 20-21 refer to the graph in Figure 2.

20. Figure 2 shows the breakdown of students' lunch orders at a cafeteria. If 120 lunches were ordered, how many students ordered pizza?

    (A) 28
    (B) 35
    (C) 36
    (D) 42
    (E) 45

21. What fraction of students ordered meatloaf or salad?

    (A) $1/10$
    (B) $1/5$
    (C) $1/4$
    (D) $2/5$
    (E) $1/2$

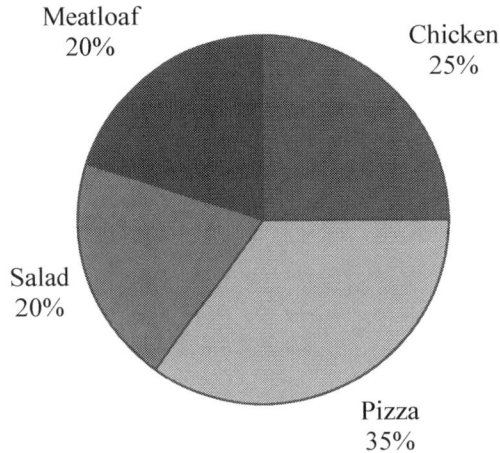

Figure 2

22. A book had an original price of G and was discounted by $3. Which expression correctly represents the final price, in dollars?

    (A) $G/3$
    (B) $3 - G$
    (C) $3G$
    (D) 3
    (E) $G - 3$

USE THIS SPACE FOR FIGURING.

23. Among the choices below, what is the largest integer?

   (A) 6
   (B) 7
   (C) 8
   (D) 9
   (E) 10

24. In Figure 3, a square with a side length of 8 is adjacent to a triangle with a base of 8. If the height of the entire figure is 10, what is its area?

   (A) 56
   (B) 64
   (C) 72
   (D) 80
   (E) It cannot be determined from the information given.

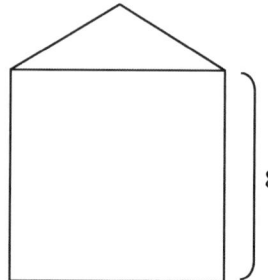

Figure 3

25. When x is multiplied by itself and 8, the product is 72. What is the value of x?

   (A) 3
   (B) 4
   (C) 5
   (D) 8
   (E) 9

STOP

IF YOU FINISH BEFORE TIME IS CALLED,
YOU MAY CHECK YOUR WORK ON THIS SECTION ONLY.
DO NOT TURN TO ANY OTHER SECTION IN THE TEST.

SECTION 2
40 Questions

Read each passage carefully and then answer the questions about it. For each question, decide on the basis of the passage which one of the choices best answers the question.

Falconry—the practice of hunting with trained birds of prey—was for many ages one of the main sports of the richer classes. Since many more efficient methods of hunting have always existed, falconry has probably always been considered a pure sport rather than a practical method of hunting. Falconry is very ancient. It was probably introduced into England from continental Europe
Line 5   about A.D. 860, and from that time to the middle of the 17th century, falconry excited more enthusiasm than has any other English sport, even fox-hunting. Stringent laws, notably during the reigns of William the Conqueror, Edward III, Henry VIII and Elizabeth, were passed from time to time to regulate falconry. Varieties of falcon and hawk were allotted to men according to rank and station—for instance, to the emperor the eagle and vulture, to royalty the jerfalcons, to an earl the peregrine, to a yeoman the
    10   goshawk, and to a servant the useless kestrel.

---

1. The main purpose of this passage is to

    (A) criticize the inefficient practice of using falcons to capture game
    (B) provide some historical information about falconry
    (C) describe sporting life under the reign of William the Conqueror
    (D) argue that falconry is the best sport
    (E) rank varieties of falcon and hawk

2. As it is used in the passage, "a pure sport" (line 3) is probably

    (A) a sport that only the wealthy engage in
    (B) a sport that is favored and regulated by British monarchs
    (C) a sport that is engaged in for entertainment and not out of necessity
    (D) a very popular sport
    (E) a very old sport

3. According to the passage, falconry most likely spread to England

    (A) in the middle of the 17th century
    (B) during the reign of Queen Elizabeth
    (C) during the reign of King Henry VIII
    (D) around A.D. 860
    (E) in order to help identify rank

4. The passage suggests that fox-hunting

    (A) has been extremely popular in England
    (B) is a cruel sport
    (C) is the most effective way of capturing game
    (D) is older than falconry
    (E) has been banned by Elizabeth II

GO ON TO THE NEXT PAGE.

5. Which of these puts the falcons and hawks in correct order of rank, from lowest to highest?

   (A) kestrel, vulture, goshawk, peregrine
   (B) eagle, peregrine, kestrel, jerfalcon
   (C) eagle, vulture, goshawk, peregrine
   (D) kestrel, peregrine, jerfalcon, eagle
   (E) kestrel, eagle, jerfalcon, vulture

GO ON TO THE NEXT PAGE.

Names should always be carefully chosen. They are apt to influence friendships or to excite prejudices according to their significance. We Chinese are very particular in this matter. When a son is born the father or the grandfather chooses a name for the infant boy which, according to his horoscope, is likely to insure him success. Hence such names as
Line 5 "happiness," "prosperity," "longevity," "success," and others are common in China. Girls' names are generally selected from flowers, fruits, or trees. Particular care is taken not to use a name which has a bad meaning. In Washington I once met a man in an elevator whose name was "Coffin." Was I to be blamed for wondering if the elevator would be my coffin? On another occasion I met a man whose name was "Death," and as soon as I heard his name I felt inclined
10 to run away, for I did not wish to die. I am not superstitious. I have frequently taken dinner with thirteen persons at the table, and I do not hesitate to start on a journey on a Friday. I often do things which would not be done by superstitious persons in China. But to meet a man calling himself "Coffin" or "Death" was too much for me, and with all my disbelief in superstition I could not help showing some aversion to those who bore such names.

6. A good title for this passage might be

   (A) A Man Named "Death"
   (B) The Importance of Names
   (C) Cultural Differences between America and China
   (D) Leaving on a Friday
   (E) The Fear of Elevators

7. As it is used in the passage, the word "insure" (line 4) most likely means

   (A) protect
   (B) guarantee
   (C) predict
   (D) highlight
   (E) prohibit

8. The speaker claims that he is

   I. from America
   II. from China
   III. always superstitious

   (A) I only
   (B) II only
   (C) I and III only
   (D) II and III only
   (E) None of these

9. When the speaker met a man named "Coffin," he was

   (A) unconcerned, although he knew that he was in danger
   (B) carefree, although he did not normally ride in elevators
   (C) frightened, although he was not normally superstitious
   (D) friendly, although he did not normally talk to strangers
   (E) furious, although he did not normally lose his temper

GO ON TO THE NEXT PAGE.

10. It can be inferred from the passage that starting a trip on a Friday

    (A) is rude to the people you dine with that night
    (B) is against the law in China
    (C) is considered by some to invite bad luck
    (D) counteracts the bad luck incurred by dining with twelve other people
    (E) means you won't reach China before Monday

GO ON TO THE NEXT PAGE.

In 1959, scientists in the Soviet Union who were interested in the process by which wolves became domesticated dogs initiated a breeding experiment using silver foxes. The experiment was led by Dmitri Belyaev.

Belyaev believed that in the ancestral past of dogs, wolves with less fear of humans were more likely to live near them and eat scraps of their food. These wolves, he thought, must have interbred, passing down their tolerance of humans to their descendants, who eventually became domestic dogs. To mimic this process, he acquired a population of silver foxes and bred only those that had "low flight distance"—that is, the ones that he could get quite close to before they ran away from him.

Since behavior is rooted in biology, by choosing foxes that behaved in a certain way, Belyaev was choosing foxes that shared certain biological traits governing that behavior. After several generations of foxes chosen for breeding based on their "flight distance," Russian scientists now have a number of domesticated foxes, the descendants of Belyaev's original population. These domestic foxes are not only more comfortable around humans than their wild forebears, but also have important physical differences, such as spotted fur and raised tails—traits that are common in domestic dogs.

11. This passage answers all of the following questions EXCEPT:

(A) During which year did Belyaev begin his silver fox experiment?
(B) Why were silver foxes chosen for the experiment rather than wolves?
(C) What did Belyaev believe was the process by which wolves became dogs?
(D) How did Belyaev choose which foxes to breed?
(E) Are there any differences between the domesticated foxes and their wild ancestors?

12. When the author states that "behavior is rooted in biology" (line 10), he most likely means that

(A) biological traits strongly influence how an animal acts
(B) eating certain plants can change an animal's temperament
(C) it is in the nature of all foxes to be fearful of humans
(D) there is no relationship between biological makeup and behavior
(E) choosing foxes to breed in the way Belyaev did will never result in changes in biology

GO ON TO THE NEXT PAGE.

13. If one of Belyaev's foxes ran away from him as soon as it noticed him, Belyaev would

    (A) sell it to the Department of Fur Animal Breeding
    (B) coax it back with rabbit meat
    (C) not use it to breed the next generation of foxes
    (D) lose track of it in the lab
    (E) breed it with a fox that had equally high "flight" distance

14. This passage suggests that Belyaev's breeding experiment

    (A) was a risky experiment
    (B) has created foxes that are somewhat dog-like
    (C) is unfair to the foxes
    (D) is almost over
    (E) failed to produce significant results

GO ON TO THE NEXT PAGE.

To buy a horse was Birt's greatest ambition. His father died; and as misfortunes seldom come singly, the horse on which the family depended to till their scanty fields died shortly after its owner. Whenever the spring arrived, their one chance to plant a crop was to hire a mule from their nearest neighbor, the tanner. Birt was the eldest son, and his mother had only his work to offer in
Line 5   payment. The tanner always greeted this proposition coldly. The mule was needed to haul up piles of bark from the depths of the woods to the tanyard. Then, too, he had his own crops to plant. Although the mule was a multifarious animal that ploughed and worked in the bark-mill, and hauled bark from the woods, and took long journeys with the wagon or under the saddle, it was impossible for her to be in all the places in which she was urgently needed at the same time. Therefore, to hire her out hardly
10   seemed to benefit her master. Nevertheless, this bargain was struck every spring. The poverty-stricken widow always congratulated herself upon it, and it never occurred to her that the amount of work that Birt did in the tanyard was more than enough payment for the few days that the tanner's mule ploughed their little fields.

15. When did Birt's family's horse die?

    (A) in the spring
    (B) before his father died
    (C) after his father died
    (D) while it was plowing the field
    (E) after Birt died

16. What deal was struck every spring?

    (A) The tanner gave Birt's mother some bark, and Birt's mother lent him their horse.
    (B) Birt drove the tanner's wagon, and the tanner helped Birt's mother in the field.
    (C) Birt gave the tanner his crops, and the tanner gave Birt's mother a horse.
    (D) The tanner lent Birt's mother his mule, and Birt did work for the tanner.
    (E) Birt hauled bark from the woods, and Birt's mother rode the tanner's mule to town.

17. What is the most likely reason that Birt's family always struck this deal in the spring?

    (A) The spring was the time of the year when they needed to till their fields to plant a crop.
    (B) Their old horse died in the spring.
    (C) The spring was the time of the year when the tanner didn't need to use the mule.
    (D) Birt was busy at home for the rest of the year.
    (E) It was too cold to walk to the tanner's house during any other time of the year.

18. The passage answers all of the following questions EXCEPT:

    (A) Did Birt have an older brother?
    (B) What did Birt's family need the mule for?
    (C) Why did the tanner need the mule?
    (D) What did Birt want more than anything?
    (E) How many siblings did Birt have?

GO ON TO THE NEXT PAGE.

19. In the last sentence of the passage (lines 10-13), the author suggests that

    (A) Birt's mother didn't really need the mule
    (B) Birt enjoyed his work for the tanner and spent as much time with him as possible
    (C) Birt's mother didn't realize that the deal with the tanner was uneven
    (D) Birt's mother was a professional bargainer
    (E) Birt worked so hard for the tanner that he gave them the mule

20. Every time Birt's mother made her yearly deal with the farmer, she felt

    (A) pleased and proud
    (B) warm-hearted and generous
    (C) foolish and mistaken
    (D) careless and forgetful
    (E) pretty and young

GO ON TO THE NEXT PAGE.

Proudly raising four fingers—representing the four stripes of the Catalan flag—the enxaneta is greeted by uproarious applause, which he or she can usually enjoy only for a moment before scrambling down the other side of the human tower known as a castell.

"Castell" is the Catalan word for, as an English-speaker might guess, "castle." Castells are a
Line 5 Catalan tradition dating back to the 18th century, when they were first built during local festivals in the city of Valls. Today, castell teams—or colles—build elaborate human towers during festivals throughout Catalonia as well as in competition.

While castell teams were traditionally all-male, today's colles are as diverse as the communities they come from, uniting men and women of all ages in a feat that is bigger than themselves. Each level
10 of the castell is formed by two to five people standing on the shoulders of those in the level below. The enxaneta is the brave soul, almost always a child, who climbs to the top of a castell to mark its completion. Then begins the treacherous process of dismantling the many levels (as many as ten) of castellers who make up the tower. But the danger is not quite as great as it might seem—hundreds of supporters form a pinya, or base, for the castell, cushioning the fall of the castellers in case of collapse.

21. A good title for this passage might be

    (A) A Brief History of Catalonia
    (B) The Journey of the Enxaneta
    (C) Castells: Human Towers of Catalonia
    (D) Castles of Spain and France
    (E) The Fight for Catalonian Independence

22. The author would probably agree with all of the following EXCEPT:

    (A) the completion of a castell is an exciting moment for the audience
    (B) today's castell teams are better than those of the 18th century
    (C) building a castell is an impressive achievement
    (D) climbing to the top of a castell seems scary
    (E) castellers are actually safer than their audience might imagine

23. Which best summarizes the history of castells and castell teams?

    (A) Building castells started in the 18th century all over Catalonia as an activity that brought men and women together.
    (B) Castells were first built by all-male teams in 18th century Valls; today, men, women, and children build them together all over Catalonia.
    (C) Castells were once popular throughout Catalonia but today are mainly built by the inhabitants of Valls.
    (D) In the 18th century, castells were mainly a children's game during festivals, but today men and women of all ages can participate.
    (E) Building castells is a new sport that was designed to heal social rifts by uniting diverse groups in pursuit of a common goal.

GO ON TO THE NEXT PAGE.

24. According to the passage, what is the role of the pinya (line 14)?

    (A) The pinya is the final layer of the castell.
    (B) The pinya is a crowd of fans that will cheer the castellers even if they fail.
    (C) If the castellers lose their balance and fall, the supporters in the pinya will help them back onto their feet.
    (D) If the castellers lose their balance and fall, they will fall safely onto the pinya instead of hitting the ground.
    (E) The pinya is the child who goes to the top of the castell to signal its completion.

25. The attitude of the author towards castells is best described as

    (A) alarmed
    (B) bored
    (C) critical
    (D) disbelieving
    (E) admiring

GO ON TO THE NEXT PAGE.

There was sarcasm in the voice. Andrew Provost resented the tone. He had never liked Mr. Raymond overmuch, though they had met on more than one planet and had dined together frequently. Besides, it raised his hackles to have his family insulted. He knew his niece to be a young woman worth trusting. If she said she could do this thing, then she could.

Line 5   "By golly, I'll give her the opportunity!" he cried.

"Your money would be wasted," Mr. Raymond replied curtly. "Build a spaceship in that time, with workers inexperienced in such an endeavor—a ship, moreover, of almost unlimited range! You are dreaming!"

"I am all seriousness," said Mr. Provost's niece. "If I had the means I would construct this ship, 10 and prove its capacity to you. It would go where you wished; no corner of the galaxy would be too far."

"And I back her up in what she says," cried Andrew warmly.

26. It can be inferred from the passage that Andrew Provost

(A) is an expert engineer
(B) has traveled widely
(C) is not particularly wealthy
(D) was once close friends with Mr. Raymond
(E) has no children of his own

27. Why does Mr. Raymond feel that the project in the passage would be a waste of money?

(A) He thinks that Mr. Provost already has enough spaceships.
(B) He thinks that space travel is impossible.
(C) He has never met Mr. Provost before.
(D) He thinks that the scope of the project is unrealistic.
(E) He thinks that spaceships are always bad investments.

28. As portrayed in the passage, Mr. Raymond might be described as

(A) friendly
(B) skeptical
(C) unreasonable
(D) fatherly
(E) optimistic

29. What is special about the ship that Mr. Provost's niece wants to build?

(A) It will be able to travel anywhere in the galaxy.
(B) It will be possible to replicate it cheaply and quickly.
(C) It will be able to carry thousands of passengers.
(D) It will withstand attack better than any other ship.
(E) It will have the capacity to become invisible.

30. This passage is most likely to be found in

(A) a history of space travel
(B) a book of traditional legends
(C) a science fiction novel
(D) a guide to building a spaceship
(E) a play about young inventors

GO ON TO THE NEXT PAGE.

When you say that a book was "meant to be read," you mean, for one thing, that it was not meant to be studied. You do not study a good story, or a haunting poem, or a battle song, or a love ballad, or any moving narrative, whether it be out of history or out of fiction. You do not have to study these things; they reveal themselves to you. They remain with you, and will
Line 5 not be forgotten. They cling like personal experience, and become the mind's close friends. You devour a book "meant to be read," not because you are anxious to be nourished, but because it contains such stuff as makes the mind hungry. Nor do you read it to kill time, but rather to lengthen time, to live more abundantly while it lasts, adding another's life and thoughts to your own.

31. Which of these would the author most likely think was NOT "meant to be read"?

    (A) a poem about memories of a long-ago time
    (B) a story about an exciting adventure
    (C) an instruction manual for a piece of equipment
    (D) a narrative about a historical figure
    (E) a novel with memorable characters

32. According to the passage, books that are "meant to be read"

    (A) are good for momentary entertainment, but will be forgotten soon after
    (B) are always fictional
    (C) must be carefully studied
    (D) make you eager to read more
    (E) contain important information

33. As used in the passage, "to live more abundantly" (line 8) most likely means

    (A) to live carefully, watching out for danger
    (B) to live richly, taking in an array of thoughts and experiences
    (C) to live dangerously, risking your life for cheap thrills
    (D) to live humbly, putting others first
    (E) to live diligently, working at every moment

34. The tone of this passage is

    (A) resentful
    (B) passionate
    (C) humorous
    (D) bored
    (E) indifferent

GO ON TO THE NEXT PAGE.

The guests arrive a little before the appointed time and enter an interior waiting room, where they store unneeded items such as coats, and put on fresh tabi—special socks worn with traditional Japanese sandals. In an alcove in the waiting room hangs a beautiful scroll with watercolors or calligraphy alluding to the season or some other appropriate theme
Line 5 for the ceremony. When all the guests have arrived and finished their preparations, they proceed to the outdoor waiting bench in a simple garden outside the teahouse, where they remain until summoned by the host.

Following a silent bow between host and guests, the guests proceed in order to a stone basin where they ritually purify themselves by washing their hands and rinsing their
10 mouths with water. They remove their sandals and enter the tea room, where they sit seiza-style on the tatami mats in order of prestige. Here, too, there is a hanging scroll in an alcove.

The chaji, or tea ceremony, begins in the cool months with the laying of the charcoal fire which will be used to heat the water. Following this, guests are served a meal in several courses accompanied by rice wine and followed by a small sweet. After the meal there is a
15 break, during which the guests return to the garden while the host replaces the scroll with a flower arrangement, opens the tea room's shutters, and makes preparations for making and serving the tea.

35. This passage is primarily about Japanese

    (A) manners
    (B) food
    (C) religion
    (D) tea ceremonies
    (E) gardens

36. According to the passage, the guests at a Japanese tea ceremony remove their sandals

    (A) before entering the waiting room
    (B) before entering the garden
    (C) before greeting their host
    (D) before entering the tea room
    (E) before washing their hands

37. The mood of a Japanese tea ceremony could best be described as

    (A) tense
    (B) casual
    (C) dark
    (D) formal
    (E) celebratory

38. This passage would likely be found in

    (A) a cookbook
    (B) a novel
    (C) a newspaper
    (D) a personal letter
    (E) a guidebook

GO ON TO THE NEXT PAGE.

39. It can be inferred from the passage that during the meal

    (A) the host is not present
    (B) the guests eat too much
    (C) the host gets very tired
    (D) the shutters of the tea room are shut
    (E) night is falling outside

40. The author will most likely continue by

    (A) comparing the Japanese tea ceremony to British high tea
    (B) explaining what is on the scrolls in greater detail
    (C) describing the next step in the tea ceremony
    (D) listing prominent figures in the history of the tea ceremony
    (E) complaining about how long and boring the tea ceremony is

STOP

IF YOU FINISH BEFORE TIME IS CALLED,
YOU MAY CHECK YOUR WORK ON THIS SECTION ONLY.
DO NOT TURN TO ANY OTHER SECTION IN THE TEST.

SECTION 3
60 Questions

This section consists of two different types of questions: synonyms and analogies. There are directions and a sample question for each type.

Synonyms

Each of the following questions consists of one word followed by five words or phrases. You are to select the one word or phrase whose meaning is closest to the word in capital letters.

Sample Question:

CHILLY:
(A) lazy
(B) nice
(C) dry
(D) cold
(E) sunny

Ⓐ Ⓑ Ⓒ ● Ⓔ

---

1. DAWDLE:
   (A) draw
   (B) delay
   (C) hurry
   (D) trip
   (E) return

2. IMMEDIATE:
   (A) news-worthy
   (B) late
   (C) prompt
   (D) invisible
   (E) unexpected

3. DISTINGUISHED:
   (A) decayed
   (B) damp
   (C) invincible
   (D) friendly
   (E) dignified

4. SOLEMN:
   (A) miserable
   (B) boring
   (C) magnificent
   (D) serious
   (E) difficult

5. BEHOLD:
   (A) cradle
   (B) observe
   (C) stop
   (D) arrest
   (E) borrow

6. VANITY:
   (A) pride
   (B) greed
   (C) ruthlessness
   (D) imagination
   (E) disobedience

GO ON TO THE NEXT PAGE.

7. MODERATE:
   (A) partisan
   (B) not extreme
   (C) not warm
   (D) careless
   (E) condescending

8. SEIZE:
   (A) attack
   (B) refuse
   (C) count
   (D) capture
   (E) destroy

9. AMBITIOUS:
   (A) bold
   (B) perfect
   (C) lazy
   (D) careful
   (E) elite

10. IMMUNITY:
    (A) disrespect
    (B) ability
    (C) protection
    (D) dirtiness
    (E) conscience

11. VAST:
    (A) empty
    (B) high
    (C) sweater
    (D) grassy
    (E) expansive

12. FORLORN:
    (A) lonely
    (B) short
    (C) evil
    (D) hidden
    (E) respectable

13. OVERWHELM:
    (A) overcook
    (B) overlook
    (C) overpower
    (D) overthink
    (E) oversee

14. ADJUST:
    (A) judge
    (B) try
    (C) carry
    (D) cease
    (E) tweak

15. SQUALL:
    (A) air
    (B) wave
    (C) storm
    (D) fish
    (E) moment

16. BURLY:
    (A) clumsy
    (B) muscular
    (C) angry
    (D) dour
    (E) sloppy

GO ON TO THE NEXT PAGE.

17. QUASH:

    (A) lull
    (B) suppress
    (C) cushion
    (D) avoid
    (E) ignore

18. INSCRUTABLE:

    (A) entertaining
    (B) affordable
    (C) mysterious
    (D) impaired
    (E) alive

19. CURTAIL:

    (A) circle
    (B) rejoice
    (C) limit
    (D) frown
    (E) mistake

20. EVADE:

    (A) murder
    (B) exile
    (C) empty
    (D) catch
    (E) escape

21. MISCHIEVOUS:

    (A) smiling
    (B) young
    (C) troublemaking
    (D) ridiculous
    (E) unwise

22. GUARANTEE:

    (A) offer
    (B) imprison
    (C) restrain
    (D) assure
    (E) dictate

23. RELENTLESS:

    (A) impure
    (B) unyielding
    (C) incomplete
    (D) soft
    (E) irrelevant

24. EXTRANEOUS:

    (A) accelerated
    (B) fascinating
    (C) uncertain
    (D) irrelevant
    (E) impudent

25. MALIGNANT:

    (A) indignant
    (B) evil
    (C) boring
    (D) frustrated
    (E) empirical

26. CIVILITY:

    (A) politeness
    (B) conflict
    (C) corruption
    (D) activism
    (E) charity

GO ON TO THE NEXT PAGE.

27. REPUGNANT:

    (A) stunted
    (B) hungry
    (C) disgusting
    (D) unlucky
    (E) insane

28. FRUITLESS:

    (A) abandoned
    (B) unproductive
    (C) ripe
    (D) protracted
    (E) undone

29. SERENITY:

    (A) madness
    (B) slumber
    (C) peace
    (D) foolishness
    (E) joy

30. CARESS:

    (A) stroke
    (B) smile
    (C) laugh
    (D) push
    (E) tap

GO ON TO THE NEXT PAGE.

Analogies

The following questions ask you to find relationships between words. For each question, select the answer choice that best completes the meaning of the sentence.

Sample Question:

> Kitten is to cat as
> (A) fawn is to colt
> (B) puppy is to dog
> (C) cow is to bull
> (D) wolf is to bear
> (E) hen is to rooster

Choice (B) is the best answer because a kitten is a young cat just as a puppy is a young dog. Of all the answer choices, (B) states a relationship that is most like the relationship between kitten and cat.

---

31. Actor is to ensemble as

    (A) captain is to crew
    (B) character is to plot
    (C) character is to play
    (D) player is to team
    (E) jockey is to horse

32. Skyscraper is to building as

    (A) bank is to supermarket
    (B) redwood is to tree
    (C) house is to home
    (D) limousine is to rowboat
    (E) sidewalk is to street

33. Lopsided is to symmetrical as

    (A) mirror is to reflection
    (B) upside-down is to flat
    (C) invisible is to ordinary
    (D) gray is to black
    (E) fractured is to whole

34. Ravenous is to hungry as

    (A) parched is to thirsty
    (B) awake is to tired
    (C) sympathetic is to concerned
    (D) pleased is to happy
    (E) reserved is to vicious

35. Recording is to voice as

    (A) microphone is to mouth
    (B) computer is to foot
    (C) scale is to body
    (D) photograph is to face
    (E) scissors are to hair

36. Dalmatian is to canine as

    (A) Yorkie is to bulldog
    (B) bird is to parrot
    (C) tabby is to feline
    (D) lion is to bear
    (E) amphibian is to reptile

GO ON TO THE NEXT PAGE.

37. Galoshes are to wet as

   (A) dress is to sunny
   (B) mittens are to cold
   (C) sponge is to water
   (D) slicker is to dry
   (E) slippers are to feet

38. Unkempt is to tidy as

   (A) sterile is to clean
   (B) unavoidable is to problematic
   (C) unschooled is to educated
   (D) consumable is to organic
   (E) liberated is to dreary

39. Paperclip is to staple as

   (A) paper is to glue
   (B) white-out is to mark
   (C) zipper is to rubber-band
   (D) pen is to cap
   (E) clips is to pierces

40. Gridlock is to traffic as

   (A) deadlock is to negotiation
   (B) wheel is to car
   (C) lock is to chain
   (D) right is to left
   (E) stoplight is to bus

41. Core is to apple as

   (A) segment is to orange
   (B) filling is to pie
   (C) fruit is to yogurt
   (D) pit is to peach
   (E) banana is to peel

42. Island is to archipelago as

   (A) boat is to canal
   (B) typewriter is to key
   (C) link is to chain
   (D) dragon is to fantasy
   (E) character is to story

43. Literary is to writing as

   (A) planetary is to traveling
   (B) culinary is to cooking
   (C) superfluous is to water
   (D) cerebral is to academic
   (E) scientific is to myth

44. Cheetah is to fast as

   (A) coyote is to industrious
   (B) dog is to friendly
   (C) blue whale is to large
   (D) hamster is to quiet
   (E) sparrow is to rare

45. Seashell is to beach as pinecone is to

   (A) desert
   (B) forest
   (C) plain
   (D) glacier
   (E) tundra

46. Canopy is to forest as

   (A) crust is to earth
   (B) tent is to jungle
   (C) mountain is to apex
   (D) atmosphere is to air
   (E) head is to shoulders

GO ON TO THE NEXT PAGE.

47. Snout is to pig as muzzle is to

   (A) rooster
   (B) mask
   (C) fish
   (D) dog
   (E) human

48. Fabricate is to make as

   (A) describe is to imagine
   (B) destroy is to build
   (C) celebrate is to create
   (D) control is to observe
   (E) disassemble is to take apart

49. Moon is to planet as planet is to

   (A) star
   (B) galaxy
   (C) world
   (D) sky
   (E) stratosphere

50. Drop is to scatter as

   (A) up is to over
   (B) down is to around
   (C) under is to through
   (D) in is to away
   (E) beside is to beneath

51. Paint is to wall as

   (A) varnish is to floor
   (B) cushion is to chair
   (C) pane is to window
   (D) drawer is to credenza
   (E) sconce is to pillar

52. Album is to song as

   (A) lyric is to music
   (B) paragraph is to text
   (C) menu is to dish
   (D) page is to novel
   (E) items is to list

53. Simplify is to complexity as

   (A) accessorize is to jewelry
   (B) vanquish is to obscurity
   (C) refine is to impurity
   (D) elect is to position
   (E) glorify is to renown

54. Month is to year as

   (A) year is to decade
   (B) day is to week
   (C) yard is to mile
   (D) inch is to foot
   (E) minute is to hour

55. Glasses are to sight as

   (A) spice is to taste
   (B) gloves are to touch
   (C) earplugs are to hearing
   (D) nose is to smell
   (E) cane is to mobility

56. Freeze is to ice as

   (A) water is to shower
   (B) frost is to snow
   (C) cold is to winter
   (D) boil is to steam
   (E) sun is to warm

GO ON TO THE NEXT PAGE.

57. Bay is to sea as

    (A) gulf is to ocean
    (B) water is to peninsula
    (C) current is to air
    (D) bridge is to bank
    (E) path is to forest

58. Summarize is to analyze as

    (A) classify is to categorize
    (B) list is to combine
    (C) record is to measure
    (D) describe is to research
    (E) shorten is to understand

59. Mumble is to speak as

    (A) chuckle is to laugh
    (B) nap is to dream
    (C) wail is to cry
    (D) grumble is to moan
    (E) snore is to sniffle

60. Slide is to stairs as

    (A) elevator is to escalator
    (B) pole is to ladder
    (C) monkey bars are to sprinkler
    (D) playground is to bank
    (E) straw is to spoon

STOP

IF YOU FINISH BEFORE TIME IS CALLED,
YOU MAY CHECK YOUR WORK ON THIS SECTION ONLY.
DO NOT TURN TO ANY OTHER SECTION IN THE TEST.

SECTION 4
25 Questions

Following each problem in this section, there are five suggested answers. Work out each problem in your head or in the blank space provided at the right of the page. Then look at the five suggested answers and decide which one is best.

Note: Figures that accompany problems in this section are drawn as accurately as possible EXCEPT when it is stated in a specific problem that its figure is not drawn to scale.

Sample problem:

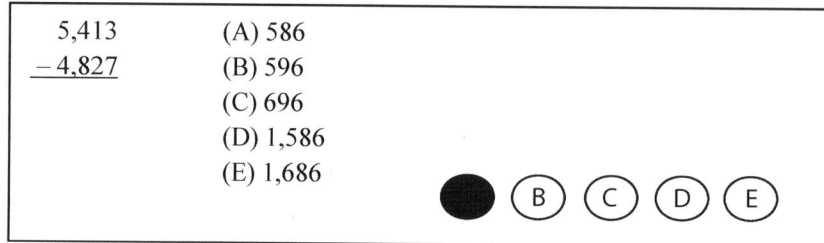

USE THIS SPACE FOR FIGURING.

1. If $A = 3$ and $B = 4$, what is the value of $A \times B$?

   (A) 1
   (B) 2
   (C) 5
   (D) 7
   (E) 12

2. $-18 + 5 =$

   (A) -23
   (B) -13
   (C) 8
   (D) 13
   (E) 23

3. Which of the following is closest to 18% of 200?

   (A) 18
   (B) 24
   (C) 28
   (D) 32
   (E) 36

GO ON TO THE NEXT PAGE.

4. Six pegs are drilled into a wooden board, and an elastic band is stretched around them so that it touches every peg. The shape formed by the elastic band could be any of the following EXCEPT

   (A) a circle
   (B) a triangle
   (C) a square
   (D) a pentagon
   (E) a hexagon

5. 3 people can pack 20 boxes in 15 minutes. If they work at the same rate, how many boxes can 6 people pack in 30 minutes?

   (A) 10
   (B) 20
   (C) 40
   (D) 60
   (E) 80

6. According to Figure 1, Author A wrote about how many more books than Author E?

   (A) 40
   (B) 50
   (C) 60
   (D) 70
   (E) 80

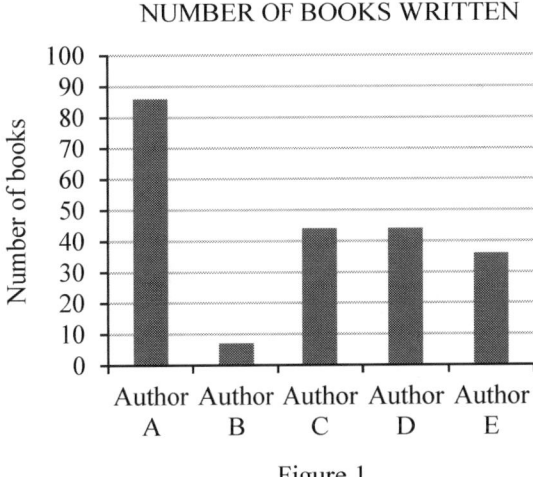

Figure 1

7. Which of the following is less than $24/7$?

   (A) $50/14$
   (B) $7/2$
   (C) $18/5$
   (D) $10/3$
   (E) $15/4$

---

8. Joann has two more cookies than Lisa. If Joann has J cookies, which of the following expressions shows the number of cookies that Lisa has?

   (A) J
   (B) $J - 2$
   (C) $J + 2$
   (D) $2J$
   (E) $J/2$

---

9. Which of the following is closest to 0.333?

   (A) $4/9$
   (B) $5/9$
   (C) $2/12$
   (D) $3/12$
   (E) $4/12$

GO ON TO THE NEXT PAGE.

10. Peter owed $140,000 to his bank. He then won a contest and received a cash prize of $250,000. He paid 50% of his prize in taxes, and he used the remaining winnings to pay off the amount he owed to the bank. How much does he still owe?

    (A) $0
    (B) $10,000
    (C) $15,000
    (D) $20,000
    (E) $25,000

11. If $R > 4$ and $S > 7$, then which of the following MUST be true?

    (A) $R \times S > 28$
    (B) $R \times S < 28$
    (C) $R \times S = 28$
    (D) $R \div S > 4 \div 7$
    (E) $R \div S < 4 \div 7$

12. If each side of a hexagon has a length of 4, what is the hexagon's perimeter?

    (A) 4
    (B) 16
    (C) 20
    (D) 24
    (E) 32

13. Ashley has a number of boxes which measure 6 × 5 × 10 inches. She wants to fill the boxes with books that are 5 inches wide, 9 inches tall, and 1.5 inches thick. What is the greatest number of books that Ashley can put in each box?

    (A) 2
    (B) 3
    (C) 4
    (D) 5
    (E) 6

14. For all real numbers j and k, $\boxed{j+k} = j^2 + k^2$.

    For example, $\boxed{2+3} = 2^2 + 3^2 = 4 + 9 = 13$.

    What is the value of $\boxed{5+10}$?

    (A) 15
    (B) 25
    (C) 100
    (D) 125
    (E) 225

15. Alice has two cartons of eggs. If a twelfth of the eggs in the first carton are cracked and a fourth of the eggs in the second carton are cracked, what is the fraction of cracked eggs in both cartons?

    (A) $1/16$
    (B) $1/12$
    (C) $1/8$
    (D) $1/6$
    (E) $1/4$

GO ON TO THE NEXT PAGE.

16. Which of these numbers can be written in the form $33k + 17$ for some whole number k?

    (A) 66,000
    (B) 66,034
    (C) 66,050
    (D) 66,066
    (E) 66,085

17. A swimming pool is being filled with water at a rate of 120 cubic feet per hour. If the pool measures 10 feet long by 12 feet wide by 8 feet deep, how long will it take for the pool to be entirely full?

    (A) 8 hrs
    (B) 12 hrs
    (C) 16 hrs
    (D) 80 hrs
    (E) 960 hrs

18. What is the next number in the sequence below?

    $$\frac{1}{3}, \frac{1}{6}, \frac{1}{12}, \frac{1}{24}, \underline{\qquad}$$

    (A) $1/36$
    (B) $1/48$
    (C) 30
    (D) 36
    (E) 48

19. Dave and Ryan spent $16 on a whole pizza. When they ate 3/4 of the pizza, they had 4 slices left over. What was the average cost per slice of pizza?

    (A) $1
    (B) $2
    (C) $5
    (D) $4
    (E) $8

20. An automobile plant can manufacture 4 cars every 90 minutes. At this rate, how many cars can be manufactured in 90 hours?

    (A) 40
    (B) 120
    (C) 200
    (D) 240
    (E) 360

21. In Figure 2, $a = 45$, $b = 35$, and $c = 50$. What is the value of d?

    (A) 40
    (B) 50
    (C) 60
    (D) 70
    (E) It cannot be determined from the information given.

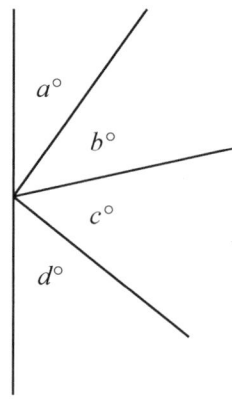

Figure 2

22. Saito has a 90cm-long strip of paper, which he wants to cut into smaller strips of equal length. Which of the following is NOT a possible length for these smaller strips?

    (A) 2 cm
    (B) 4 cm
    (C) 5 cm
    (D) 15 cm
    (E) 18 cm

23. In Figure 3, an equilateral triangle with a side length of 3 is placed on top of a square with a side length of 5. What is the perimeter of the whole figure?

    (A) 21
    (B) 22
    (C) 23
    (D) 26
    (E) 29

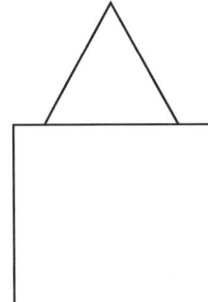

Figure 3

24. A bank has 24 security guards. One third of the security guards work a night shift. How many security guards do NOT work a night shift?

    (A) 6
    (B) 8
    (C) 12
    (D) 16
    (E) 18

25. If $5 + 4N = 29$, then $N =$

    (A) 5
    (B) 5.25
    (C) 6
    (D) 6.25
    (E) 7

STOP

IF YOU FINISH BEFORE TIME IS CALLED,
YOU MAY CHECK YOUR WORK ON THIS SECTION ONLY.
DO NOT TURN TO ANY OTHER SECTION IN THE TEST.

Upper Level
Practice Test 3

How to Take this Practice Test

To simulate an accurate testing environment, sit at a desk in a quiet location free of distractions—no TV, computers, phones, music, or noise—and clear your desk of all materials except pencils and erasers. Remember that no calculators, rulers, protractors, dictionaries, or other aids are allowed on the SSAT.

Give yourself the following amounts of time for each section:

Section	Subject	Time Limit
	Writing	25 minutes
	5-minute break	
1	Math I	30 minutes
2	Reading	40 minutes
	5-minute break	
3	Verbal	30 minutes
4	Math II	30 minutes

Have an adult help you monitor your time, or use a stopwatch and time yourself. Only give yourself the allotted time for each section; put your pencil down when your time is up. Note: timing may be extended for students with diagnosed learning disabilities who apply for testing with accommodations.

Follow the instructions carefully. As you take your test, bubble your answers into the answer sheets provided. Use the test booklet as scratch paper for notes and calculations. Remember that you are not granted time at the end of a section to transfer your answers to the answer sheet, so you must do this as you go along.

When you are finished, check your answers against the answer keys provided. Then, score your exam using the directions at the end.

Be sure each mark completely fills the answer space.
Start with number 1 for each new section of the test. You may find more answer spaces than you need. If so, please leave them blank.

SECTION 1

1. Ⓐ Ⓑ Ⓒ Ⓓ Ⓔ
2. Ⓐ Ⓑ Ⓒ Ⓓ Ⓔ
3. Ⓐ Ⓑ Ⓒ Ⓓ Ⓔ
4. Ⓐ Ⓑ Ⓒ Ⓓ Ⓔ
5. Ⓐ Ⓑ Ⓒ Ⓓ Ⓔ
6. Ⓐ Ⓑ Ⓒ Ⓓ Ⓔ
7. Ⓐ Ⓑ Ⓒ Ⓓ Ⓔ
8. Ⓐ Ⓑ Ⓒ Ⓓ Ⓔ
9. Ⓐ Ⓑ Ⓒ Ⓓ Ⓔ
10. Ⓐ Ⓑ Ⓒ Ⓓ Ⓔ
11. Ⓐ Ⓑ Ⓒ Ⓓ Ⓔ
12. Ⓐ Ⓑ Ⓒ Ⓓ Ⓔ
13. Ⓐ Ⓑ Ⓒ Ⓓ Ⓔ
14. Ⓐ Ⓑ Ⓒ Ⓓ Ⓔ
15. Ⓐ Ⓑ Ⓒ Ⓓ Ⓔ
16. Ⓐ Ⓑ Ⓒ Ⓓ Ⓔ
17. Ⓐ Ⓑ Ⓒ Ⓓ Ⓔ
18. Ⓐ Ⓑ Ⓒ Ⓓ Ⓔ
19. Ⓐ Ⓑ Ⓒ Ⓓ Ⓔ
20. Ⓐ Ⓑ Ⓒ Ⓓ Ⓔ
21. Ⓐ Ⓑ Ⓒ Ⓓ Ⓔ
22. Ⓐ Ⓑ Ⓒ Ⓓ Ⓔ
23. Ⓐ Ⓑ Ⓒ Ⓓ Ⓔ
24. Ⓐ Ⓑ Ⓒ Ⓓ Ⓔ
25. Ⓐ Ⓑ Ⓒ Ⓓ Ⓔ

SECTION 2

1. Ⓐ Ⓑ Ⓒ Ⓓ Ⓔ
2. Ⓐ Ⓑ Ⓒ Ⓓ Ⓔ
3. Ⓐ Ⓑ Ⓒ Ⓓ Ⓔ
4. Ⓐ Ⓑ Ⓒ Ⓓ Ⓔ
5. Ⓐ Ⓑ Ⓒ Ⓓ Ⓔ
6. Ⓐ Ⓑ Ⓒ Ⓓ Ⓔ
7. Ⓐ Ⓑ Ⓒ Ⓓ Ⓔ
8. Ⓐ Ⓑ Ⓒ Ⓓ Ⓔ
9. Ⓐ Ⓑ Ⓒ Ⓓ Ⓔ
10. Ⓐ Ⓑ Ⓒ Ⓓ Ⓔ
11. Ⓐ Ⓑ Ⓒ Ⓓ Ⓔ
12. Ⓐ Ⓑ Ⓒ Ⓓ Ⓔ
13. Ⓐ Ⓑ Ⓒ Ⓓ Ⓔ
14. Ⓐ Ⓑ Ⓒ Ⓓ Ⓔ
15. Ⓐ Ⓑ Ⓒ Ⓓ Ⓔ
16. Ⓐ Ⓑ Ⓒ Ⓓ Ⓔ
17. Ⓐ Ⓑ Ⓒ Ⓓ Ⓔ
18. Ⓐ Ⓑ Ⓒ Ⓓ Ⓔ
19. Ⓐ Ⓑ Ⓒ Ⓓ Ⓔ
20. Ⓐ Ⓑ Ⓒ Ⓓ Ⓔ
21. Ⓐ Ⓑ Ⓒ Ⓓ Ⓔ
22. Ⓐ Ⓑ Ⓒ Ⓓ Ⓔ
23. Ⓐ Ⓑ Ⓒ Ⓓ Ⓔ
24. Ⓐ Ⓑ Ⓒ Ⓓ Ⓔ
25. Ⓐ Ⓑ Ⓒ Ⓓ Ⓔ
26. Ⓐ Ⓑ Ⓒ Ⓓ Ⓔ
27. Ⓐ Ⓑ Ⓒ Ⓓ Ⓔ
28. Ⓐ Ⓑ Ⓒ Ⓓ Ⓔ
29. Ⓐ Ⓑ Ⓒ Ⓓ Ⓔ
30. Ⓐ Ⓑ Ⓒ Ⓓ Ⓔ
31. Ⓐ Ⓑ Ⓒ Ⓓ Ⓔ
32. Ⓐ Ⓑ Ⓒ Ⓓ Ⓔ
33. Ⓐ Ⓑ Ⓒ Ⓓ Ⓔ
34. Ⓐ Ⓑ Ⓒ Ⓓ Ⓔ
35. Ⓐ Ⓑ Ⓒ Ⓓ Ⓔ
36. Ⓐ Ⓑ Ⓒ Ⓓ Ⓔ
37. Ⓐ Ⓑ Ⓒ Ⓓ Ⓔ
38. Ⓐ Ⓑ Ⓒ Ⓓ Ⓔ
39. Ⓐ Ⓑ Ⓒ Ⓓ Ⓔ
40. Ⓐ Ⓑ Ⓒ Ⓓ Ⓔ

SECTION 3

1. Ⓐ Ⓑ Ⓒ Ⓓ Ⓔ
2. Ⓐ Ⓑ Ⓒ Ⓓ Ⓔ
3. Ⓐ Ⓑ Ⓒ Ⓓ Ⓔ
4. Ⓐ Ⓑ Ⓒ Ⓓ Ⓔ
5. Ⓐ Ⓑ Ⓒ Ⓓ Ⓔ
6. Ⓐ Ⓑ Ⓒ Ⓓ Ⓔ
7. Ⓐ Ⓑ Ⓒ Ⓓ Ⓔ
8. Ⓐ Ⓑ Ⓒ Ⓓ Ⓔ
9. Ⓐ Ⓑ Ⓒ Ⓓ Ⓔ
10. Ⓐ Ⓑ Ⓒ Ⓓ Ⓔ
11. Ⓐ Ⓑ Ⓒ Ⓓ Ⓔ
12. Ⓐ Ⓑ Ⓒ Ⓓ Ⓔ
13. Ⓐ Ⓑ Ⓒ Ⓓ Ⓔ
14. Ⓐ Ⓑ Ⓒ Ⓓ Ⓔ
15. Ⓐ Ⓑ Ⓒ Ⓓ Ⓔ
16. Ⓐ Ⓑ Ⓒ Ⓓ Ⓔ
17. Ⓐ Ⓑ Ⓒ Ⓓ Ⓔ
18. Ⓐ Ⓑ Ⓒ Ⓓ Ⓔ
19. Ⓐ Ⓑ Ⓒ Ⓓ Ⓔ
20. Ⓐ Ⓑ Ⓒ Ⓓ Ⓔ
21. Ⓐ Ⓑ Ⓒ Ⓓ Ⓔ
22. Ⓐ Ⓑ Ⓒ Ⓓ Ⓔ
23. Ⓐ Ⓑ Ⓒ Ⓓ Ⓔ
24. Ⓐ Ⓑ Ⓒ Ⓓ Ⓔ
25. Ⓐ Ⓑ Ⓒ Ⓓ Ⓔ
26. Ⓐ Ⓑ Ⓒ Ⓓ Ⓔ
27. Ⓐ Ⓑ Ⓒ Ⓓ Ⓔ
28. Ⓐ Ⓑ Ⓒ Ⓓ Ⓔ
29. Ⓐ Ⓑ Ⓒ Ⓓ Ⓔ
30. Ⓐ Ⓑ Ⓒ Ⓓ Ⓔ
31. Ⓐ Ⓑ Ⓒ Ⓓ Ⓔ
32. Ⓐ Ⓑ Ⓒ Ⓓ Ⓔ
33. Ⓐ Ⓑ Ⓒ Ⓓ Ⓔ
34. Ⓐ Ⓑ Ⓒ Ⓓ Ⓔ
35. Ⓐ Ⓑ Ⓒ Ⓓ Ⓔ
36. Ⓐ Ⓑ Ⓒ Ⓓ Ⓔ
37. Ⓐ Ⓑ Ⓒ Ⓓ Ⓔ
38. Ⓐ Ⓑ Ⓒ Ⓓ Ⓔ
39. Ⓐ Ⓑ Ⓒ Ⓓ Ⓔ
40. Ⓐ Ⓑ Ⓒ Ⓓ Ⓔ
41. Ⓐ Ⓑ Ⓒ Ⓓ Ⓔ
42. Ⓐ Ⓑ Ⓒ Ⓓ Ⓔ
43. Ⓐ Ⓑ Ⓒ Ⓓ Ⓔ
44. Ⓐ Ⓑ Ⓒ Ⓓ Ⓔ
45. Ⓐ Ⓑ Ⓒ Ⓓ Ⓔ
46. Ⓐ Ⓑ Ⓒ Ⓓ Ⓔ
47. Ⓐ Ⓑ Ⓒ Ⓓ Ⓔ
48. Ⓐ Ⓑ Ⓒ Ⓓ Ⓔ
49. Ⓐ Ⓑ Ⓒ Ⓓ Ⓔ
50. Ⓐ Ⓑ Ⓒ Ⓓ Ⓔ
51. Ⓐ Ⓑ Ⓒ Ⓓ Ⓔ
52. Ⓐ Ⓑ Ⓒ Ⓓ Ⓔ
53. Ⓐ Ⓑ Ⓒ Ⓓ Ⓔ
54. Ⓐ Ⓑ Ⓒ Ⓓ Ⓔ
55. Ⓐ Ⓑ Ⓒ Ⓓ Ⓔ
56. Ⓐ Ⓑ Ⓒ Ⓓ Ⓔ
57. Ⓐ Ⓑ Ⓒ Ⓓ Ⓔ
58. Ⓐ Ⓑ Ⓒ Ⓓ Ⓔ
59. Ⓐ Ⓑ Ⓒ Ⓓ Ⓔ
60. Ⓐ Ⓑ Ⓒ Ⓓ Ⓔ

SECTION 4

1. Ⓐ Ⓑ Ⓒ Ⓓ Ⓔ
2. Ⓐ Ⓑ Ⓒ Ⓓ Ⓔ
3. Ⓐ Ⓑ Ⓒ Ⓓ Ⓔ
4. Ⓐ Ⓑ Ⓒ Ⓓ Ⓔ
5. Ⓐ Ⓑ Ⓒ Ⓓ Ⓔ
6. Ⓐ Ⓑ Ⓒ Ⓓ Ⓔ
7. Ⓐ Ⓑ Ⓒ Ⓓ Ⓔ
8. Ⓐ Ⓑ Ⓒ Ⓓ Ⓔ
9. Ⓐ Ⓑ Ⓒ Ⓓ Ⓔ
10. Ⓐ Ⓑ Ⓒ Ⓓ Ⓔ
11. � Ⓑ Ⓒ Ⓓ Ⓔ
12. Ⓐ Ⓑ Ⓒ Ⓓ Ⓔ
13. Ⓐ Ⓑ Ⓒ Ⓓ Ⓔ
14. Ⓐ Ⓑ Ⓒ Ⓓ Ⓔ
15. Ⓐ Ⓑ Ⓒ Ⓓ Ⓔ
16. Ⓐ Ⓑ Ⓒ Ⓓ Ⓔ
17. Ⓐ Ⓑ Ⓒ Ⓓ Ⓔ
18. Ⓐ Ⓑ Ⓒ Ⓓ Ⓔ
19. Ⓐ Ⓑ Ⓒ Ⓓ Ⓔ
20. Ⓐ Ⓑ Ⓒ Ⓓ Ⓔ
21. Ⓐ Ⓑ Ⓒ Ⓓ Ⓔ
22. Ⓐ Ⓑ Ⓒ Ⓓ Ⓔ
23. Ⓐ Ⓑ Ⓒ Ⓓ Ⓔ
24. Ⓐ Ⓑ Ⓒ Ⓓ Ⓔ
25. � Ⓑ Ⓒ Ⓓ Ⓔ

Practice Test 3: Upper Level

Writing Sample

Schools would like to get to know you better through a story you tell using one of the ideas below. Please choose the idea you find most interesting and write a story using the idea as your first sentence. Please fill in the circle next to the one you choose.

(A) If you could relive a particular moment, what would it be and why?

(B) She looked up and gasped.

Use this page and the next page to complete your writing sample.

Continue on next page

SECTION 1

25 Questions

Following each problem in this section, there are five suggested answers. Work out each problem in your head or in the blank space provided at the right of the page. Then look at the five suggested answers and decide which one is best.

Note: Figures that accompany problems in this section are drawn as accurately as possible EXCEPT when it is stated in a specific problem that its figure is not drawn to scale.

Sample problem:

5,413	(A) 586
− 4,827	(B) 596
	(C) 696
	(D) 1,586
	(E) 1,686

● Ⓑ Ⓒ Ⓓ Ⓔ

USE THIS SPACE FOR FIGURING.

1. When 9206 is divided by 180, the remainder is

    (A) 26
    (B) 39
    (C) 42
    (D) 51
    (E) 56

2. $3/4 + 0.34 =$

    (A) 0.34
    (B) 0.43
    (C) 0.68
    (D) 1.09
    (E) 2.68

GO ON TO THE NEXT PAGE.

3. Which of the following is a whole number?

   (A) −2.5
   (B) $106/3$
   (C) 33%
   (D) $108/3$
   (E) 1.25

4. In Figure 1, two congruent regular pentagons are joined at the base. If the perimeter of the entire figure is 40, each pentagon must have a side length of

   (A) 4
   (B) 5
   (C) 8
   (D) 10
   (E) 16

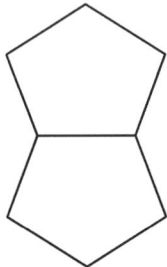

Figure 1

5. According to Figure 2, what were the approximate average earnings of the three highest-grossing films during the weekend of July 13-15?

   (A) $20 million
   (B) $30 million
   (C) $40 million
   (D) $50 million
   (E) $80 million

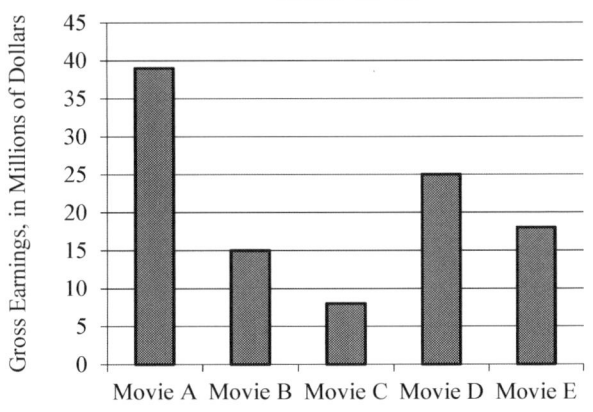

Figure 2

GO ON TO THE NEXT PAGE.

6. If $N \div 2 = 14$, then $N \div 4 =$

    (A) 2
    (B) 6
    (C) 7
    (D) 14
    (E) 28

---

7. $\frac{1}{4}\left(\frac{1}{2}\right) + \frac{1}{16} =$

    (A) $1/32$
    (B) $2/16$
    (C) $3/16$
    (D) $2/8$
    (E) $1/2$

---

8. If $N + 2 > 2$, then which of the following MUST be true?

    (A) $N > 0$
    (B) $N + 1 < 2$
    (C) $N + 1 > 2$
    (D) $N > 1$
    (E) $N = 2$

---

9. A train took between $2\frac{1}{4}$ and $2\frac{1}{2}$ hours to complete a 150 mile trip. What was the train's average speed, in miles per hour?

    (A) 50
    (B) 59
    (C) 62
    (D) 67
    (E) 75

GO ON TO THE NEXT PAGE.

10. How many small cubes with a side length of 1 meter can fit in a larger cube with a side length of 5 meters?

    (A) 5
    (B) 10
    (C) 25
    (D) 125
    (E) 200

11. Ms. Jarwahl owns one apartment that measures 60 feet by 40 feet. She also owns a second apartment that measures 30 feet by 90 feet. What is the average square footage of the two apartments?

    (A) 2400 ft^2
    (B) 2450 ft^2
    (C) 2550 ft^2
    (D) 2700 ft^2
    (E) 3200 ft^2

12. Which of the following numbers can be written in the form $7C + 2$, if C is an integer?

    (A) 36
    (B) 44
    (C) 52
    (D) 60
    (E) 68

13. Kathy has replaced all of her incandescent light bulbs with fluorescent light bulbs that last 8 times longer. Compared with how frequently Kathy had to change her incandescent light bulbs previously, she will now have to change her new light bulbs

    (A) 8% as frequently
    (B) 12.5% as frequently
    (C) 15% as frequently
    (D) 80% as frequently
    (E) 92% as frequently

GO ON TO THE NEXT PAGE.

14. If one fourth of the height of a giraffe is 5 ft., three fifths of the giraffe's height is

    (A) 4 ft.
    (B) 5 ft.
    (C) 8 ft.
    (D) 10 ft.
    (E) 12 ft.

---

15. Which of the following shapes can be drawn without retracing or lifting your pencil?

    A)

    (B)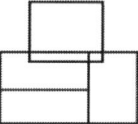

    (C)

    (D)

    (E)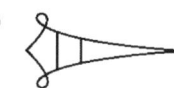

---

16. Harvey has a loan of $1,000, for which he pays about $9.88 in interest every month. This monthly interest is $1/12$ of his yearly interest. What is Harvey's yearly interest rate on his $1,000 loan?

    (A) 0.83%
    (B) 4.62%
    (C) 9.88%
    (D) 10.98%
    (E) 11.86%

GO ON TO THE NEXT PAGE.

17. In Figure 3, two parallel lines are intersected by a third line. If $x = 110$, what is the value of y?

    (A) 60
    (B) 70
    (C) 80
    (D) 110
    (E) It cannot be determined from the information given.

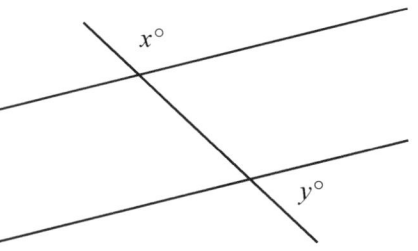

Figure 3

18. To share the cost of a gift equally, three people would each have to contribute $4. If five friends decided to share the cost of this gift equally, how much would each friend need to contribute?

    (A) $1.00
    (B) $2.00
    (C) $2.25
    (D) $2.40
    (E) $4.00

19. If a is an integer, which of the following is greatest in value?

    (A) $a/2$
    (B) $a/3$
    (C) $2a$
    (D) $3a$
    (E) It cannot be determined from the information given.

GO ON TO THE NEXT PAGE.

20. Points *A*, *B*, *C*, *D*, and *E* lie along a straight line, in that order. The distance between *A* and *B* is 5, and the distance between *C* and E is 4. The distance between *B* and *D* is 2. If the distance between *A* and *E* is 10, what is the distance between *A* and *C*?

    (A) 1
    (B) 2
    (C) 4
    (D) 5
    (E) 6

21. What is the next number in the following sequence?

    $$3, 6, 12, 24, 48, \_\_\_$$

    (A) 60
    (B) 64
    (C) 72
    (D) 84
    (E) 96

22. The organizers of a relay race are sending 3 buses to pick up runners and take them to the race site. There are 3 runners on each team, and all members of each team must travel together on the same bus. If each bus can seat 20 runners, then how many total teams can fit into the 3 buses?

    (A) 15
    (B) 16
    (C) 18
    (D) 20
    (E) 21

GO ON TO THE NEXT PAGE.

23. $AB + C6 = DE0$

Each of the five letters in the equation above stands for one of the following digits: 1, 2, 4, 5, and 6. If each letter stands for a different digit, which letter stands for the digit 2?

(A) A
(B) B
(C) C
(D) D
(E) E

24. Total sales, s, is proportional to the number of goods sold, n, and a constant price, p. Which of the following correctly represents the value of n in terms of s and p?

(A) $n = s/p$
(B) $n = p/s$
(C) $p = n/s$
(D) $p = ns$
(E) $n = sp$

25. If $\dfrac{a}{b}$ is divisible by 6, which of the following must also be divisible by 6?

(A) $\dfrac{a}{2b}$
(B) $\dfrac{2a}{b}$
(C) $\dfrac{a+b}{b}$
(D) $\dfrac{a-b}{c}$
(E) $\dfrac{a}{a+b}$

STOP

IF YOU FINISH BEFORE TIME IS CALLED,
YOU MAY CHECK YOUR WORK ON THIS SECTION ONLY.
DO NOT TURN TO ANY OTHER SECTION IN THE TEST.

SECTION 2
40 Questions

Read each passage carefully and then answer the questions about it. For each question, decide on the basis of the passage which one of the choices best answers the question.

There they sat, nearly thirty of them, on the rough benches, their faces shading from a pale cream to a deep brown, the little feet bare and swinging, the eyes full of expectation, with here and there a twinkle of mischief, and the hands grasping Webster's blue-back spelling-book. I loved my school, and the fine faith the children had in my wisdom as their teacher was truly marvelous. We read
Line 5 and spelled together, wrote a little, picked flowers, sang, and listened to stories of the world beyond the hill. At times the school would dwindle away, and I would start out. I would visit the Eddings, who lived in two very dirty rooms, and ask why little Lugene, whose flaming face seemed ever ablaze with the dark-red hair uncombed, was absent all last week, or why the unmistakable rags of Mack and Ed were so often missing. Then their father would tell me how the crops needed the boys, and their mother
10 would assure me that Lugene must mind the baby. "But we'll start them again next week." When the Lawrences stopped, I knew that the doubts of the old folks about book-learning had conquered again, and so, toiling up the hill, I put Cicero's "pro Archia Poeta" into the simplest English, and usually convinced them—for a week or so.

1. How did the speaker feel about his job at the school?

    (A) He enjoyed having such easy and entertaining work.
    (B) He resented the fact that his students didn't appreciate his expertise.
    (C) He was bored by the simple activities he had to engage in with his students.
    (D) He was proud of his school and worked hard to maintain it.
    (E) He was tired and eager to quit.

2. According to the passage, when school attendance was low the speaker would

    (A) pay social calls to while away the time
    (B) visit his students' families to find out why they were missing school
    (C) read British poetry to his students in their homes
    (D) entertain his students and their families with stories about history
    (E) recruit new students

GO ON TO THE NEXT PAGE.

3. What reasons do the Eddings give for their children's absence from school?

    (A) The children are being kept home as a punishment.
    (B) The children are needed at home to help with the farm and family.
    (C) The parents don't want their children to be seen by their classmates.
    (D) The parents don't want their children to become more educated.
    (E) The children don't enjoy school and prefer to stay home.

4. It can be inferred from the passage that Cicero's "pro Archia Poeta" (line 12) is

    (A) a Latin treatise about farming
    (B) a short story describing the benefits of studying geography
    (C) a homework assignment that the speaker's students had not completed
    (D) a poem about the uneducated
    (E) not written in simple English

GO ON TO THE NEXT PAGE.

The following is an excerpt from a speech by former United States President Lyndon B. Johnson.

Each year more than 100,000 high school graduates, with proved ability, do not enter college because they cannot afford it. And if we cannot educate today's youth, what will we do in 1970 when elementary school enrollment will be 5 million greater than 1960?

In many places, classrooms are overcrowded and curricula are outdated. Most of our qualified
Line 5 teachers are underpaid, and many of our paid teachers are unqualified. So we must give every child a place to sit and a teacher to learn from. Poverty must not be a bar to learning, and learning must offer an escape from poverty.

But more classrooms and more teachers are not enough. We must seek an educational system which grows in excellence as it grows in size. This means better training for our
10 teachers. It means preparing youth to enjoy their hours of leisure as well as their hours of labor. It means exploring new techniques of teaching, to find new ways to stimulate the love of learning and the capacity for creation.

---

5. What is the main message of this passage?

   (A) We must replace poor teachers with better ones.
   (B) Poverty is a serious problem in today's society.
   (C) We must improve the educational system.
   (D) There are too many children in the educational system.
   (E) Teaching is a very difficult career.

6. This passage was most likely written

   (A) in 1940
   (B) in 1950
   (C) in 1960
   (D) in 1970
   (E) in 1980

7. The speaker identifies all of the following as problems for the educational system, EXCEPT:

   (A) the rising cost of early-childhood education
   (B) overcrowding in schools
   (C) low pay for teachers
   (D) the high cost of a college education
   (E) curricula that contain out-of-date information

8. When the speaker says "poverty must not be a bar to learning" (line 6), he is implying that

   (A) poverty is like a ruler that measures potential in school
   (B) impoverished students have fewer educational opportunities
   (C) poverty has no effect on education
   (D) impoverished families live too far away from schools
   (E) poverty is the primary reason that students have unqualified teachers

GO ON TO THE NEXT PAGE.

9. The speaker would most likely agree that

   (A) not everyone should attend college
   (B) most teachers lack qualifications
   (C) hiring more teachers will solve all of the problems in the education system
   (D) students should work harder in school
   (E) children learn better when they enjoy learning

10. The tone of the passage is

    (A) condescending
    (B) mournful
    (C) wrathful
    (D) emphatic
    (E) sarcastic

GO ON TO THE NEXT PAGE.

Sometimes geography can affect language in surprising ways.

On the island of La Gomera—one of the Canary Islands off the cost of West Africa—deep ravines separate slivers of mountain terrain and the people who live on it. But the inhabitants of La Gomera developed a unique way of communicating across these deep
Line 5 ravines: an amazing whistled speech called Silbo Gomero. This whistled language is indigenous to the island, and its existence has been documented since Roman times. Invented by the original inhabitants of the island, the Guanches, Silbo Gomero was adopted by the Spanish settlers in the 16th century and survived after the Guanches' population dwindled. When this unique means of communication was threatened with extinction at the dawn of the
10 21st century, the local government added it to the school curriculum.

The modern language of Silbo Gomero is actually a dialect of Spanish. The Guanches originally converted the sounds of their own language into whistle-sounds, but eventually applied that practice to the language of the Spanish colonists. It is this whistled language that the Spaniards themselves adopted.

11. The primary subject of this passage is

   (A) the geography of La Gomera
   (B) the Spanish occupation of the Canary Islands
   (C) geography's relationship to language
   (D) Silbo Gomero, the whistled language of La Gomera
   (E) languages that involve whistling and other non-vocal sounds

12. According to the passage, Silbo Gomero
   I. is at least as old as the Roman Empire
   II. has evolved into a whistled dialect of Spanish
   III. has been taught in schools in La Gomera

   (A) I only
   (B) II only
   (C) III only
   (D) I and II only
   (E) I, II and III

13. Silbo Gomero was developed by the inhabitants of La Gomera so they could

   (A) plot against the Spanish colonists
   (B) communicate better in their terrain
   (C) communicate with Spanish settlers
   (D) enhance La Gomera's unique culture
   (E) communicate more privately with one another

14. How did the Spanish acquire Silbo Gomero?

   (A) They learned it in the schools of La Gomera.
   (B) They were the original settlers of La Gomera and invented the language.
   (C) They converted the Guanches' whistle sounds into their own Spanish language.
   (D) They picked up the whistled form of Spanish that the Guanches had invented.
   (E) They began whistling in order to communicate better with the Guanches.

GO ON TO THE NEXT PAGE.

15. It can be inferred that La Gomera's ravines

    (A) were detrimental to the family units of La Gomera
    (B) helped give rise to a new language
    (C) caused conflict among the inhabitants
    (D) confused the Spanish colonists
    (E) developed after people settled on La Gomera

Children have the strangest adventures without being troubled by them. For instance, they may remember to mention, a week after the event happened, that when they were in the wood they had met their dead father and played a game with him. It was in this casual way that Wendy one morning made a worrying revelation. Some leaves of a tree had been found on the nursery floor, which certainly were not there when the children went to bed, and Mrs. Darling was puzzling over them when Wendy said with a tolerant smile:

"I do believe it is that Peter again!"

"Whatever do you mean, Wendy?"

"It is so naughty of him not to wipe his feet," Wendy said, sighing. She was a tidy child. She explained in quite a matter-of-fact way that she thought Peter sometimes came to the nursery in the night and sat on the foot of her bed and played on his pipes to her. Unfortunately she never woke, so she didn't know how she knew, she just knew.

"What nonsense you talk, precious. No one can get into the house without knocking."

"I think he comes in by the window," she said.

"My love, it is three floors up."

"Were not the leaves at the foot of the window, mother?"

It was quite true; the leaves had been found very near the window.

Mrs. Darling did not know what to think, for it all seemed so natural to Wendy that you could not dismiss it by saying she had been dreaming.

"My child," the mother cried, "why did you not tell me of this before?"

"I forgot," said Wendy lightly. She was in a hurry to get her breakfast.

Oh, surely she must have been dreaming.

16. According to the passage, Wendy believes that Peter

    (A) is her father
    (B) is a character in a book
    (C) is responsible for the leaves on the floor
    (D) knocks on the front door every night
    (E) eats breakfast with her every morning

17. Mrs. Darling could best be described as

    (A) erudite
    (B) severe
    (C) perplexed
    (D) gullible
    (E) anguished

18. Wendy's attitude towards Peter could be described as

    (A) frankly astonished
    (B) mildly exasperated
    (C) secretly frightened
    (D) quietly proud
    (E) absolutely smitten

19. Without changing the author's meaning, you could replace the word "natural" (line 18) with which of the following words?

    (A) woodsy
    (B) carefree
    (C) normal
    (D) unavoidable
    (E) complicated

GO ON TO THE NEXT PAGE.

20. The narrator would most likely agree with which of the following statements?

    (A) Children tend to exaggerate.
    (B) Children often perceive imaginary events as real.
    (C) Children frequently play tricks on their parents.
    (D) Children have a faulty and undeveloped memory.
    (E) Children's dreams are sporadic.

A green leaf is green because of the presence of a pigment known as chlorophyll, but chlorophyll is not the only pigment in a leaf. Leaves also contain carotenoids, yellow and orange pigments that are present in the leaf throughout its life, and anthocyanins, red and purple pigments that develop under certain conditions in the late summer. As long as the leaf
Line 5 has plenty of chlorophyll, green will be the dominant color.

Chlorophyll has a vital function: it captures solar rays and utilizes the resulting energy to manufacture the plant's food—simple sugars that are produced from water and carbon dioxide gas and are the sole source of the carbohydrates the plant needs for growth and development. Throughout the spring and summer, the plant continually replenishes the
10 chlorophyll in its leaves so that they can keep producing its food.

In late summer, as daylight hours shorten and temperatures cool, the veins that carry fluids into and out of the leaf are gradually closed off as a layer of special cork cells forms at the base of each leaf. As this cork layer develops, the flow of chlorophyll into the leaf decreases, slowly at first, and then rapidly. Eventually, the flow of the replacement
15 chlorophyll cannot keep pace with the rate at which the chlorophyll is used up, and the leaf begins to change colors. Without the chlorophyll there to mask them, the yellow, orange, red and purple colors of the other leaf-pigments begin to show through.

21. According to the passage, chlorophyll is responsible for

    I. all pigmentation in a plant's leaves
    II. processing solar energy to create the plant's food
    III. converting a plant's carbon dioxide into water

    (A) I only
    (B) II only
    (C) II and III only
    (D) I and III only
    (E) I, II, and III

22. According to the passage, a leaf's supply of chlorophyll is replenished by

    (A) the formation of cork cells at the base of each leaf
    (B) water condensation from the atmosphere
    (C) the production of carbohydrates
    (D) veins that transport fluids into each leaf
    (E) solar rays

23. Red, yellow, and purple leaf pigments reveal themselves

    (A) during the process of photosynthesis
    (B) on cloudy days
    (C) when a leaf needs carbon dioxide
    (D) when a leaf has more chlorophyll
    (E) when a leaf has less chlorophyll

GO ON TO THE NEXT PAGE.

24. To what question might this passage be the answer?

    (A) What are the functions of chlorophyll, carotenoids and anthocyanins?
    (B) How do plants feed themselves?
    (C) Why are leaves green, and why do they change color?
    (D) What causes the seasons to change?
    (E) Why are some trees always green?

25. According to the passage, carotenoids produce which of the following colors?

    (A) yellow and orange
    (B) green
    (C) red and purple
    (D) yellow and purple
    (E) orange and red

GO ON TO THE NEXT PAGE.

> It may be misery not to sing at all
> And to go silent through the brimming day.
> It may be sorrow never to be loved,
> But deeper griefs than these beset the way.
>
> Line 5 To have come near to sing the perfect song
> And only by a half-tone lost the key,
> There is the potent sorrow, there the grief,
> The pale, sad staring of life's tragedy.
>
> This, this it is to be accursed indeed;
> 10 For if we mortals love, or if we sing,
> We count our joys not by the things we have,
> But by what kept us from the perfect thing.

26. Which of these best sums up the main idea of the poem?

    (A) It is better to have loved and lost than never to have loved at all.
    (B) Life's greatest sorrow is to come near to a great thing and never reach it.
    (C) Perfection in everything is the speaker's one ambition.
    (D) Happy is the person who can be content without love.
    (E) Life's greatest joy is to find true love, because true love lasts forever.

27. Throughout the poem, the speaker compares love to

    (A) a bird
    (B) immortality
    (C) a tragedy
    (D) singing
    (E) perfection

28. The tone of this poem could be described as

    (A) cynical
    (B) reflective
    (C) morose
    (D) angry
    (E) contemptuous

29. Based on the speaker's opinion in the poem, which of these would be worse than never pursuing a desire to become a painter?

    (A) being a very good painter, but not quite a great painter
    (B) becoming a singer instead
    (C) painting every day, but keeping your paintings to yourself
    (D) having your paintings praised by others, but not liking them yourself
    (E) never pursuing a love interest

GO ON TO THE NEXT PAGE.

Wireless reports this evening indicate that the Cunarder Carpathia reached the position from which distress calls were sent out by the Titanic last night after her collision with an iceberg. The Carpathia found there the remains and lifeboats of what had been the largest steamship in service.

The sinking of the Titanic occurred at about 2:20a.m. All her boats have been found and around 655 survivors have been rescued. About 2,100 crew members and passengers were traveling on the Titanic.

While the Leyland liner California continues to search the location of the wreckage, the Carpathia is bringing the survivors back to New York.

News of the disaster was first received 10:25 last night by wireless, and the ship continued to signal until a last blurred signal was sent and ended abruptly at 12:27a.m. Until that time, the operator's signals were perfectly clear and steady. He remained level-headed throughout and exercised the best possible judgment.

30. It can be inferred from the passage that the Olympic, the Carpathia, and the California are
    (A) icebergs
    (B) helicopters
    (C) rescue workers
    (D) ships
    (E) hotels

31. This passage would most likely be found in
    (A) an encyclopedia
    (B) a memoir
    (C) a newspaper
    (D) a film script
    (E) a letter

32. The "boats" mentioned in line 4 are probably
    (A) lifeboats used to rescue the passengers and crew
    (B) rescue boats from the Carpathia
    (C) fishing boats from the surrounding area
    (D) armed boats that defended the Titanic
    (E) the Olympic, the Carpathia, and the California

33. According to the passage, all of the following is true EXCEPT:
    (A) the last signals from the Titanic were received not long after midnight
    (B) the Leyland liner California returned to New York with all the survivors
    (C) at the time of writing, about 1,445 people from aboard the ship were unaccounted for
    (D) the Titanic wired calls for help starting at 10:25 p.m.
    (E) the Titanic sank at about 2:20 a.m.

GO ON TO THE NEXT PAGE.

34. The passage's tone when describing the Titanic's wireless operator (lines 9-11) suggests that the author considers him to be

(A) foolish
(B) unkind
(C) ignorant
(D) admirable
(E) generous

Henri Marie Raymond de Toulouse-Lautrec-Monfa—or more simply, Henri de Toulouse-Lautrec—was a French painter and illustrator whose immersion in the colorful life of Paris in the last decades of the 19th century yielded a collection of exciting, elegant and provocative images. Henri owed his long name to his aristocratic heritage, to which he also owed his serious life-long health problems. Henri's parents, the Count and Countess of
Line 5   Toulouse and Lautrec, were first cousins, and Henri suffered from health conditions often found in the offspring of close relatives. At the age of 13, Henri fractured his right thigh bone, and at 14, his left. The breaks did not heal properly, and his legs ceased to grow, so that as an adult he was just over five feet tall, having developed an adult-sized torso while retaining his child-sized legs. Physically unable to participate in many activities typically enjoyed by men of his age, Henri immersed himself in art.

10   Under the tutelage of Bonnat and later Fernand Cormon, Henri developed his vivid, characterful painting style and his taste for the Paris social scene that was so often his subject. He was masterly at capturing crowd scenes in which the figures are highly individualized. Along with Cézanne, Van Gogh, and Gauguin, Henri Toulouse-Lautrec is now known as one of the greatest painters of the period.

35. Based on the description in the passage, the paintings of Henri de Toulouse-Lautrec are most likely

   (A) drab
   (B) abstract
   (C) visionary
   (D) satirical
   (E) vibrant

36. The author states that Henri's long name and physical ailments were both a result of

   (A) malnutrition as a child
   (B) his talent as a painter
   (C) his lack of athletic ability
   (D) his aristocratic origins
   (E) his imaginative parents

37. The author suggests that Henri's masterpieces

   (A) were inspired by his engagement in the social life of his city
   (B) were successful due to his family's influence
   (C) cured him of his disabilities
   (D) allowed him to keep living the life of an aristocrat
   (E) surpassed his family's low expectations

38. According to the passage, Henri's health problems

   (A) forced him to become an artist because there were no other careers open to him
   (B) prevented him from enjoying certain experiences with his peers
   (C) directly caused his death
   (D) were common among artists in Paris during this period
   (E) raised his social status

GO ON TO THE NEXT PAGE.

39. Which of the following does the author consider one of Henri's greatest strengths as a painter?

    (A) his inspiring biography
    (B) his innovative use of color and texture
    (C) his ability to provoke a viewer's imagination through his illustrations
    (D) his memorable appearance
    (E) his ability to portray individual people within a crowd

40. Based on the information in the passage, Fernand Comon was most likely

    (A) one of Henri's childhood friends
    (B) an art critic
    (C) one of Henri's relatives
    (D) an art teacher
    (E) Henri's patron

STOP

IF YOU FINISH BEFORE TIME IS CALLED,
YOU MAY CHECK YOUR WORK ON THIS SECTION ONLY.
DO NOT TURN TO ANY OTHER SECTION IN THE TEST.

SECTION 3
60 Questions

This section consists of two different types of questions: synonyms and analogies. There are directions and a sample question for each type.

Synonyms

Each of the following questions consists of one word followed by five words or phrases. You are to select the one word or phrase whose meaning is closest to the word in capital letters.

Sample Question:

> CHILLY:
> (A) lazy
> (B) nice
> (C) dry
> (D) cold
> (E) sunny
>
> Ⓐ Ⓑ Ⓒ ● Ⓔ

---

1. EVADE:
   (A) depart
   (B) defend
   (C) escape
   (D) dislike
   (E) descend

2. SPRUCE:
   (A) broom
   (B) cleanliness
   (C) virtue
   (D) flavor
   (E) evergreen

3. FRIVOLOUS:
   (A) enjoyable
   (B) silly
   (C) outrageous
   (D) unseemly
   (E) unkempt

4. PARTRIDGE:
   (A) musical score
   (B) wood fowl
   (C) ripe fruit
   (D) wreath
   (E) mountaintop

5. DEDUCE:
   (A) lessen
   (B) tutor
   (C) demote
   (D) decline
   (E) infer

6. APPLICABLE:
   (A) submissive
   (B) appropriate
   (C) open
   (D) apprehensive
   (E) handy

GO ON TO THE NEXT PAGE.

7. VOLUNTEER:
   (A) offer
   (B) undergo
   (C) gift
   (D) chatter
   (E) limit

8. FROLIC:
   (A) hike
   (B) disembark
   (C) cavort
   (D) hoodwink
   (E) inundate

9. SYNCHRONIZE:
   (A) wind
   (B) record
   (C) measure
   (D) unify
   (E) color

10. CRUDE:
    (A) naked
    (B) insolent
    (C) unrefined
    (D) colorful
    (E) exacting

11. APPREHEND:
    (A) charge
    (B) sentence
    (C) handcuff
    (D) understand
    (E) photograph

12. JUVENILE:
    (A) imprisoned
    (B) green
    (C) joyful
    (D) innovative
    (E) healthy

13. WIRED:
    (A) crackling
    (B) catered
    (C) remote
    (D) excited
    (E) summoned

14. ANTAGONIZE:
    (A) bury a relative
    (B) celebrate a holiday
    (C) crush an insect
    (D) introduce a theme
    (E) make an enemy

15. REGENERATION:
    (A) denial
    (B) agreement
    (C) great-great-grandparents
    (D) restoration
    (E) recrimination

16. HEEDLESS:
    (A) hungry
    (B) open
    (C) reckless
    (D) remorseless
    (E) headstrong

GO ON TO THE NEXT PAGE.

17. ASSIMILATE:
    (A) anticipate
    (B) reject
    (C) incorporate
    (D) raise
    (E) return

18. REGIMEN:
    (A) plan
    (B) team
    (C) election
    (D) hunger
    (E) argument

19. ASSENT:
    (A) justify
    (B) prove
    (C) cultivate
    (D) approve
    (E) ponder

20. SKULK:
    (A) sneak
    (B) cry
    (C) blossom
    (D) run
    (E) swim

21. ABHOR:
    (A) tend
    (B) expel
    (C) criticize
    (D) loathe
    (E) demean

22. IRASCIBLE:
    (A) grumpy
    (B) unstylish
    (C) immoral
    (D) motivated
    (E) insane

23. TROUNCE:
    (A) denounce
    (B) rout
    (C) fish
    (D) captivate
    (E) capture

24. BRAND:
    (A) oats
    (B) finance
    (C) bravery
    (D) store
    (E) mark

25. RENDITION:
    (A) refrain
    (B) article
    (C) version
    (D) song
    (E) collection

26. INSIPID:
    (A) dull
    (B) tasty
    (C) liquid
    (D) invasive
    (E) isolated

GO ON TO THE NEXT PAGE.

27. ONEROUS:

(A) exceedingly difficult
(B) constantly rowdy
(C) very decisive
(D) completely united
(E) entirely mythical

28. HOIST:

(A) drop
(B) plow
(C) lift
(D) strain
(E) lever

29. HEAP:

(A) compost
(B) roll
(C) rake
(D) bury
(E) pile

30. LIVID:

(A) vivacious
(B) life-long
(C) disappointed
(D) furious
(E) verbose

GO ON TO THE NEXT PAGE.

Analogies

The following questions ask you to find relationships between words. For each question, select the answer choice that best completes the meaning of the sentence.

Sample Question:

> Kitten is to cat as
>
> (A) fawn is to colt
> (B) puppy is to dog
> (C) cow is to bull
> (D) wolf is to bear
> (E) hen is to rooster

Choice (B) is the best answer because a kitten is a young cat just as a puppy is a young dog. Of all the answer choices, (B) states a relationship that is most like the relationship between kitten and cat.

---

31. Scissors are to paper as

    (A) string is to box
    (B) glue is to clippings
    (C) knife is to butter
    (D) hatchet is to lumberjack
    (E) pencil is to sharpener

32. Gum is to stick as

    (A) wad is to money
    (B) ice is to cube
    (C) spice is to taste
    (D) bubble is to branch
    (E) chocolate is to wrapper

33. Pathetic is to pity as awesome is to

    (A) warmth
    (B) pride
    (C) cool
    (D) boredom
    (E) amazement

34. Inter is to tomb as

    (A) steeple is to cathedral
    (B) shroud is to mourn
    (C) bury is to body
    (D) deposit is to bank
    (E) interval is to entomb

35. Dam is to river as

    (A) speculation is to concept
    (B) reckoning is to analysis
    (C) filibuster is to vote
    (D) analysis is to confusion
    (E) mother is to bay

36. Hour is to watch as

    (A) pound is to scale
    (B) minute is to second
    (C) hourglass is to clock
    (D) thermometer is to fever
    (E) day is to year

GO ON TO THE NEXT PAGE.

37. Wind is to whistle as

    (A) hum is to heaven
    (B) brook is to babble
    (C) leaf is to laugh
    (D) grass is to giggle
    (E) shore is to shout

38. Doctor is to health as

    (A) actor is to theater
    (B) cartoonist is to funny
    (C) personal trainer is to fitness
    (D) philosopher is to truth
    (E) plumber is to toilet

39. Cross is to angry as

    (A) droll is to funny
    (B) dull is to smiling
    (C) firm is to feeble
    (D) young is to touchy
    (E) healthy is to agreeable

40. Vivacious is to lively as

    (A) fertile is to pretty
    (B) loquacious is to talkative
    (C) gargantuan is to cheerful
    (D) insane is to normal
    (E) tranquil is to wild

41. Ravioli is to dumpling as

    (A) taco is to shell
    (B) rice is to soup
    (C) chocolate is to cake
    (D) mint is to lollipop
    (E) spaghetti is to noodle

42. Gravity is to force as

    (A) levity is to humorous
    (B) oxygen is to element
    (C) pathogen is to illness
    (D) electricity is to magnetism
    (E) hearing is to vibration

43. Impound is to property as

    (A) impersonate is to officer
    (B) imprison is to person
    (C) profound is to theory
    (D) resounding is to success
    (E) employ is to subordinate

44. Password is to account as

    (A) identity is to individual
    (B) number is to phone
    (C) bank is to secret
    (D) watchword is to lookout
    (E) key is to house

45. Insolence is to brazen as

    (A) rebellion is to cautious
    (B) obedience is to dutiful
    (C) insulin is to sugar
    (D) contempt is to submission
    (E) humble is to servant

46. Careless is to neglect as

    (A) sloppy is to work
    (B) untidy is to workplace
    (C) cruel is to punishment
    (D) malicious is to sabotage
    (E) objective is to plan

GO ON TO THE NEXT PAGE.

47. Inhospitable is to welcoming as unbearable is to

    (A) colorful
    (B) picturesque
    (C) lamentable
    (D) enjoyable
    (E) ridiculous

48. Utopia is to location as

    (A) European is to continental
    (B) euphoria is to sensation
    (C) unified is to disparate
    (D) enthusiastic is to salutation
    (E) myopia is to place

49. Caricature is to person as

    (A) parody is to artwork
    (B) criticism is to movie
    (C) derision is to joke
    (D) rejection is to offer
    (E) admiration is to hero

50. Tie is to neck as

    (A) seatbelt is to car
    (B) shoe is to lace
    (C) coat is to arm
    (D) sash is to waist
    (E) button is to shirt

51. Varied is to identical as

    (A) collaborative is to unilateral
    (B) reticent is to hesitant
    (C) joyous is to serious
    (D) mysterious is to friendly
    (E) exotic is to alike

52. Hibernate is to nap as

    (A) den is to bedroom
    (B) sun is to moon
    (C) gorge is to nibble
    (D) some are to all
    (E) spontaneous is to temporary

53. Effervescent is to bubbles as

    (A) courageous is to fire
    (B) expedient is to embers
    (C) curtailed is to seeds
    (D) reminiscent is to roses
    (E) scintillating is to sparkles

54. Recall is to memory as

    (A) ignore is to feeling
    (B) connect is to meeting
    (C) listen is to anecdote
    (D) suppose is to speculation
    (E) pursue is to dream

55. Excavate is to dig as

    (A) investigate is to listen
    (B) evacuate is to empty
    (C) control is to order
    (D) discover is to mystify
    (E) orient is to map

56. Cactus is to plant as

    (A) snake is to reptile
    (B) necklace is to jewelry
    (C) porcupine is to animal
    (D) hydrangea is to flower
    (E) amethyst is to gem

GO ON TO THE NEXT PAGE.

57. Plutocrat is to opulent as
    (A) farmer is to farming
    (B) messenger is to swift
    (C) democrat is to democracy
    (D) soldier is to salutary
    (E) beggar is to destitute

58. Palatial is to space as
    (A) labyrinthine is to corridors
    (B) somber is to mood
    (C) character is to morality
    (D) insomniac is to sleep
    (E) sorry is to wrong

59. Problem is to calamity as
    (A) happiness is to cheer
    (B) luck is to veracity
    (C) meal is to banquet
    (D) discovery is to calumny
    (E) animosity is to dislike

60. Pugnacious is to fight as
    (A) gluttonous is to eat
    (B) voracious is to read
    (C) contagious is to vomit
    (D) courageous is to succeed
    (E) compatible is to compete

STOP

IF YOU FINISH BEFORE TIME IS CALLED,
YOU MAY CHECK YOUR WORK ON THIS SECTION ONLY.
DO NOT TURN TO ANY OTHER SECTION IN THE TEST.

SECTION 4
25 Questions

Following each problem in this section, there are five suggested answers. Work out each problem in your head or in the blank space provided at the right of the page. Then look at the five suggested answers and decide which one is best.

Note: Figures that accompany problems in this section are drawn as accurately as possible EXCEPT when it is stated in a specific problem that its figure is not drawn to scale.

Sample problem:

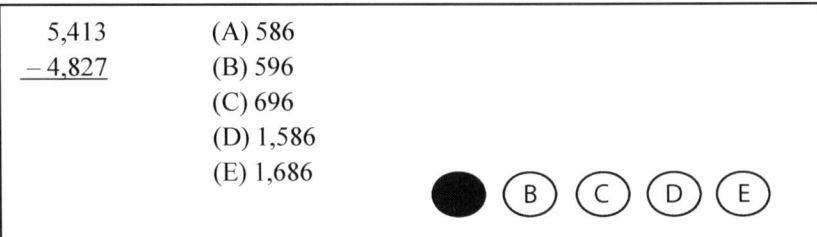

USE THIS SPACE FOR FIGURING.

1. John has x erasers more than Ed. If Ed has 10 erasers, how many erasers does John have?

    (A) $10x$
    (B) $x + 10$
    (C) $10 - x$
    (D) $10 \div x$
    (E) 10

2. The quotient of 63 divided by 7 is

    (A) 6
    (B) 7
    (C) 8
    (D) 9
    (E) 63

GO ON TO THE NEXT PAGE.

3. Ariel has $7.75 and Javier has $10.25. How much money does Javier need to give Ariel for each to have the same amount?

   (A) $0.75
   (B) $1.25
   (C) $1.75
   (D) $2.50
   (E) $9.00

4. $\frac{1}{4} + \frac{4}{1} =$

   (A) $\frac{4}{5}$
   (B) $\frac{5}{5}$
   (C) $\frac{5}{4}$
   (D) 4
   (E) $\frac{17}{4}$

5. 3.562 is closest in value to

   (A) 3.526
   (B) 3.560
   (C) 3.563
   (D) 3.625
   (E) 3.652

6. 12 is 5 percent of

   (A) 0.6
   (B) 6
   (C) 24
   (D) 60
   (E) 240

7. If Matthias bikes eight miles in half an hour, what is his average speed?

    (A) 2 mph
    (B) 4 mph
    (C) 8 mph
    (D) 16 mph
    (E) 24 mph

8. If $0.25 \times N = 4N$, then $N =$

    (A) 0
    (B) 1
    (C) 4
    (D) 16
    (E) It cannot be determined from the information given.

9. A T-shirt is on sale for 25% off of the regular price of $15.99. About how much less is the sale price than the regular price?

    (A) $3
    (B) $4
    (C) $8
    (D) $9
    (E) $12

10. Mr. Bouchard is building fences around two rectangular fields. One field measures 120 feet by 200 feet, and the other field measures 160 feet by 100 feet. If the two fields are not adjacent, how many feet of fencing will Mr. Bouchard need to surround both fields?

    (A) 900
    (B) 1050
    (C) 1100
    (D) 1160
    (E) 1200

GO ON TO THE NEXT PAGE.

11. If $2/3 + M < 1/6$, which of the following could be a value for M?

    (A) $-2/3$
    (B) $-1/2$
    (C) $-1/3$
    (D) $1/3$
    (E) $2/3$

12. Gabrielle has packed 15 pieces of clothing for a vacation, but has only $3/4$ of the clothes she will need. How many more pieces of clothing does she need to pack?

    (A) 5
    (B) 6
    (C) 7
    (D) 8
    (E) 9

13. According to the graph in Figure 1, pencil production increased at the greatest rate between which years?

    (A) 1990-1994
    (B) 1994-1998
    (C) 1998-2002
    (D) 2002-2006
    (E) 2006-2010

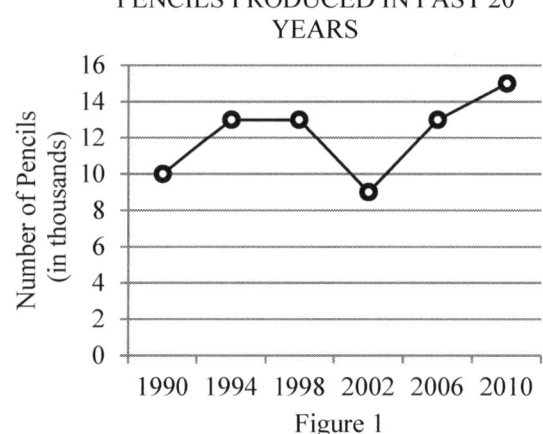

Figure 1

14. The sum of three consecutive odd integers is 27. What is the smallest of the three integers?

    (A) 3
    (B) 5
    (C) 7
    (D) 11
    (E) 15

15. Cindy is 4 years older than Sally, and Sally is twice as old as Nicole. If Cindy is 18, how old is Nicole?

    (A) 4
    (B) 7
    (C) 9
    (D) 11
    (E) 14

16. In a school picnic, a total of 43 students brought a backpack, a lunchbox, or both a backpack and a lunchbox. If there are a total of 23 backpacks and 25 lunchboxes, how many students brought both a backpack and a lunchbox?

    (A) 5
    (B) 7
    (C) 10
    (D) 17
    (E) 20

GO ON TO THE NEXT PAGE.

Questions 17 and 18 refer to the following definition.

For all real numbers p and q, $p \square q = p + (p + 1) + pq$.

For example, $2 \square 3 = 2 + (2 + 1) + 2 \times 3 = 11$.

17. What is the value of $4 \square 6$?

    (A) 24
    (B) 33
    (C) 34
    (D) 35
    (E) 40

18. If $M \square N = 4$, which of the following statements MUST be false?

    (A) M is a whole number.
    (B) N is equal to zero.
    (C) M is equal to zero.
    (D) M is an odd number.
    (E) M is equal to N.

19. 30% of $\frac{1}{4}x$ is equal to $\frac{1}{3}$ of 27. What is the value of x?

    (A) 3
    (B) 27
    (C) 80
    (D) 90
    (E) 120

20. What is the distance between Point A (–5, 2) and Point B (3, –4)?

    (A) 6
    (B) 7
    (C) 8
    (D) 9
    (E) 10

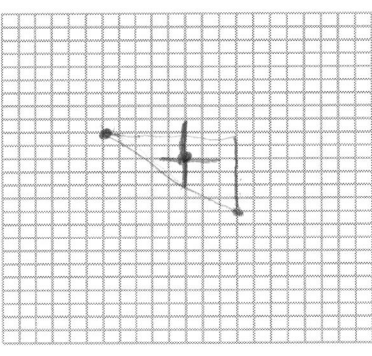

21. The price of a stock increased $1.25 on Monday, decreased $0.50 on Tuesday, stayed the same on Wednesday, increased $2.30 on Thursday, and decreased $0.45 on Friday. The price on Friday was how much greater than the price on Monday?

    (A) $2.30
    (B) $2.60
    (C) $2.70
    (D) $3.05
    (E) $3.70

22. Kurt has g one-hundred dollar bills, h twenty dollar bills, and two dollars. Which of the following expressions represents his total amount of money, in dollars?

    (A) $g + h + 2$
    (B) $\frac{g}{100} + \frac{h}{20} + 2$
    (C) $20g + 100h + 2$
    (D) $100g + 20h + 2$
    (E) It cannot be determined from the information given.

23. In Figure 3 (not drawn to scale), a semicircle with an area of 12 intersects a triangle. If $x = 90$, what is the area of the shaded region?

    (A) 4
    (B) 6
    (C) 8
    (D) 9
    (E) 12

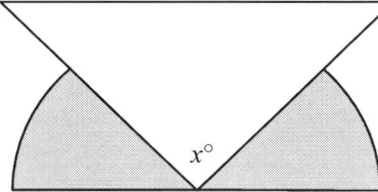

Figure 3

GO ON TO THE NEXT PAGE.

USE THIS SPACE FOR FIGURING.

24. When a pie is cut into sevenths instead of eighths, which of the following is true?

    (A) The slices are smaller.
    (B) There is one more slice.
    (C) There is one less slice.
    (D) The slices are the same size.
    (E) The slices are not the same shape.

---

25. 5 athletes competed on a team in a relay race, where each athlete ran 1 lap around a track. Catherine and William averaged 87 seconds per lap. Elizabeth, Rufus, and Henry averaged 97 seconds per lap. When all 5 laps were complete, what was the team's total time?

    (A) 455 seconds
    (B) 460 seconds
    (C) 465 seconds
    (D) 470 seconds
    (E) 475 seconds

STOP

IF YOU FINISH BEFORE TIME IS CALLED,
YOU MAY CHECK YOUR WORK ON THIS SECTION ONLY.
DO NOT TURN TO ANY OTHER SECTION IN THE TEST.

Upper Level
Practice Test 4

How to Take this Practice Test

To simulate an accurate testing environment, sit at a desk in a quiet location free of distractions—no TV, computers, phones, music, or noise—and clear your desk of all materials except pencils and erasers. Remember that no calculators, rulers, protractors, dictionaries, or other aids are allowed on the SSAT.

Give yourself the following amounts of time for each section:

Section	Subject	Time Limit
	Writing	25 minutes
	5-minute break	
1	Math I	30 minutes
2	Reading	40 minutes
	5-minute break	
3	Verbal	30 minutes
4	Math II	30 minutes

Have an adult help you monitor your time, or use a stopwatch and time yourself. Only give yourself the allotted time for each section; put your pencil down when your time is up. Note: timing may be extended for students with diagnosed learning disabilities who apply for testing with accommodations.

Follow the instructions carefully. As you take your test, bubble your answers into the answer sheets provided. Use the test booklet as scratch paper for notes and calculations. Remember that you are not granted time at the end of a section to transfer your answers to the answer sheet, so you must do this as you go along.

When you are finished, check your answers against the answer keys provided. Then, score your exam using the directions at the end.

Be sure each mark completely fills the answer space.

Start with number 1 for each new section of the test. You may find more answer spaces than you need. If so, please leave them blank.

SECTION 1

1. Ⓐ Ⓑ Ⓒ Ⓓ Ⓔ	6. Ⓐ Ⓑ Ⓒ Ⓓ Ⓔ	11. Ⓐ Ⓑ Ⓒ Ⓓ Ⓔ	16. Ⓐ Ⓑ Ⓒ Ⓓ Ⓔ	21. Ⓐ Ⓑ Ⓒ Ⓓ Ⓔ
2. Ⓐ Ⓑ Ⓒ Ⓓ Ⓔ	7. Ⓐ Ⓑ Ⓒ Ⓓ Ⓔ	12. Ⓐ Ⓑ Ⓒ Ⓓ Ⓔ	17. Ⓐ Ⓑ Ⓒ Ⓓ Ⓔ	22. Ⓐ Ⓑ Ⓒ Ⓓ Ⓔ
3. Ⓐ Ⓑ Ⓒ Ⓓ Ⓔ	8. Ⓐ Ⓑ Ⓒ Ⓓ Ⓔ	13. Ⓐ Ⓑ Ⓒ Ⓓ Ⓔ	18. Ⓐ Ⓑ Ⓒ Ⓓ Ⓔ	23. Ⓐ Ⓑ Ⓒ Ⓓ Ⓔ
4. Ⓐ Ⓑ Ⓒ Ⓓ Ⓔ	9. Ⓐ Ⓑ Ⓒ Ⓓ Ⓔ	14. Ⓐ Ⓑ Ⓒ Ⓓ Ⓔ	19. Ⓐ Ⓑ Ⓒ Ⓓ Ⓔ	24. Ⓐ Ⓑ Ⓒ Ⓓ Ⓔ
5. Ⓐ Ⓑ Ⓒ Ⓓ Ⓔ	10. Ⓐ Ⓑ Ⓒ Ⓓ Ⓔ	15. Ⓐ Ⓑ Ⓒ Ⓓ Ⓔ	20. Ⓐ Ⓑ Ⓒ Ⓓ Ⓔ	25. Ⓐ Ⓑ Ⓒ Ⓓ Ⓔ

SECTION 2

1. Ⓐ Ⓑ Ⓒ Ⓓ Ⓔ	9. Ⓐ Ⓑ Ⓒ Ⓓ Ⓔ	17. Ⓐ Ⓑ Ⓒ Ⓓ Ⓔ	25. Ⓐ Ⓑ Ⓒ Ⓓ Ⓔ	33. Ⓐ Ⓑ Ⓒ Ⓓ Ⓔ
2. Ⓐ Ⓑ Ⓒ Ⓓ Ⓔ	10. Ⓐ Ⓑ Ⓒ Ⓓ Ⓔ	18. Ⓐ Ⓑ Ⓒ Ⓓ Ⓔ	26. Ⓐ Ⓑ Ⓒ Ⓓ Ⓔ	34. Ⓐ Ⓑ Ⓒ Ⓓ Ⓔ
3. Ⓐ Ⓑ Ⓒ Ⓓ Ⓔ	11. Ⓐ Ⓑ Ⓒ Ⓓ Ⓔ	19. Ⓐ Ⓑ Ⓒ Ⓓ Ⓔ	27. Ⓐ Ⓑ Ⓒ Ⓓ Ⓔ	35. Ⓐ Ⓑ Ⓒ Ⓓ Ⓔ
4. Ⓐ Ⓑ Ⓒ Ⓓ Ⓔ	12. Ⓐ Ⓑ Ⓒ Ⓓ Ⓔ	20. Ⓐ Ⓑ Ⓒ Ⓓ Ⓔ	28. Ⓐ Ⓑ Ⓒ Ⓓ Ⓔ	36. Ⓐ Ⓑ Ⓒ Ⓓ Ⓔ
5. Ⓐ Ⓑ Ⓒ Ⓓ Ⓔ	13. Ⓐ Ⓑ Ⓒ Ⓓ Ⓔ	21. Ⓐ Ⓑ Ⓒ Ⓓ Ⓔ	29. Ⓐ Ⓑ Ⓒ Ⓓ Ⓔ	37. Ⓐ Ⓑ Ⓒ Ⓓ Ⓔ
6. Ⓐ Ⓑ Ⓒ Ⓓ Ⓔ	14. Ⓐ Ⓑ Ⓒ Ⓓ Ⓔ	22. Ⓐ Ⓑ Ⓒ Ⓓ Ⓔ	30. Ⓐ Ⓑ Ⓒ Ⓓ Ⓔ	38. Ⓐ Ⓑ Ⓒ Ⓓ Ⓔ
7. Ⓐ Ⓑ Ⓒ Ⓓ Ⓔ	15. Ⓐ Ⓑ Ⓒ Ⓓ Ⓔ	23. Ⓐ Ⓑ Ⓒ Ⓓ Ⓔ	31. Ⓐ Ⓑ Ⓒ Ⓓ Ⓔ	39. Ⓐ Ⓑ Ⓒ Ⓓ Ⓔ
8. Ⓐ Ⓑ Ⓒ Ⓓ Ⓔ	16. Ⓐ Ⓑ Ⓒ Ⓓ Ⓔ	24. Ⓐ Ⓑ Ⓒ Ⓓ Ⓔ	32. Ⓐ Ⓑ Ⓒ Ⓓ Ⓔ	40. Ⓐ Ⓑ Ⓒ Ⓓ Ⓔ

SECTION 3

1. Ⓐ Ⓑ Ⓒ Ⓓ Ⓔ	13. Ⓐ Ⓑ Ⓒ Ⓓ Ⓔ	25. Ⓐ Ⓑ Ⓒ Ⓓ Ⓔ	37. Ⓐ Ⓑ Ⓒ Ⓓ Ⓔ	49. Ⓐ Ⓑ Ⓒ Ⓓ Ⓔ
2. Ⓐ Ⓑ Ⓒ Ⓓ Ⓔ	14. Ⓐ Ⓑ Ⓒ Ⓓ Ⓔ	26. Ⓐ Ⓑ Ⓒ Ⓓ Ⓔ	38. Ⓐ Ⓑ Ⓒ Ⓓ Ⓔ	50. Ⓐ Ⓑ Ⓒ Ⓓ Ⓔ
3. Ⓐ Ⓑ Ⓒ Ⓓ Ⓔ	15. Ⓐ Ⓑ Ⓒ Ⓓ Ⓔ	27. Ⓐ Ⓑ Ⓒ Ⓓ Ⓔ	39. Ⓐ Ⓑ Ⓒ Ⓓ Ⓔ	51. Ⓐ Ⓑ Ⓒ Ⓓ Ⓔ
4. Ⓐ Ⓑ Ⓒ Ⓓ Ⓔ	16. Ⓐ Ⓑ Ⓒ Ⓓ Ⓔ	28. Ⓐ Ⓑ Ⓒ Ⓓ Ⓔ	40. Ⓐ Ⓑ Ⓒ Ⓓ Ⓔ	52. Ⓐ Ⓑ Ⓒ Ⓓ Ⓔ
5. Ⓐ Ⓑ Ⓒ Ⓓ Ⓔ	17. Ⓐ Ⓑ Ⓒ Ⓓ Ⓔ	29. Ⓐ Ⓑ Ⓒ Ⓓ Ⓔ	41. Ⓐ Ⓑ Ⓒ Ⓓ Ⓔ	53. Ⓐ Ⓑ Ⓒ Ⓓ Ⓔ
6. Ⓐ Ⓑ Ⓒ Ⓓ Ⓔ	18. Ⓐ Ⓑ Ⓒ Ⓓ Ⓔ	30. Ⓐ Ⓑ Ⓒ Ⓓ Ⓔ	42. Ⓐ Ⓑ Ⓒ Ⓓ Ⓔ	54. Ⓐ Ⓑ Ⓒ Ⓓ Ⓔ
7. Ⓐ Ⓑ Ⓒ Ⓓ Ⓔ	19. Ⓐ Ⓑ Ⓒ Ⓓ Ⓔ	31. Ⓐ Ⓑ Ⓒ Ⓓ Ⓔ	43. Ⓐ Ⓑ Ⓒ Ⓓ Ⓔ	55. Ⓐ Ⓑ Ⓒ Ⓓ Ⓔ
8. Ⓐ Ⓑ Ⓒ Ⓓ Ⓔ	20. Ⓐ Ⓑ Ⓒ Ⓓ Ⓔ	32. Ⓐ Ⓑ Ⓒ Ⓓ Ⓔ	44. Ⓐ Ⓑ Ⓒ Ⓓ Ⓔ	56. Ⓐ Ⓑ Ⓒ Ⓓ Ⓔ
9. Ⓐ Ⓑ Ⓒ Ⓓ Ⓔ	21. Ⓐ Ⓑ Ⓒ Ⓓ Ⓔ	33. Ⓐ Ⓑ Ⓒ Ⓓ Ⓔ	45. Ⓐ Ⓑ Ⓒ Ⓓ Ⓔ	57. Ⓐ Ⓑ Ⓒ Ⓓ Ⓔ
10. Ⓐ Ⓑ Ⓒ Ⓓ Ⓔ	22. Ⓐ Ⓑ Ⓒ Ⓓ Ⓔ	34. Ⓐ Ⓑ Ⓒ Ⓓ Ⓔ	46. Ⓐ Ⓑ Ⓒ Ⓓ Ⓔ	58. Ⓐ Ⓑ Ⓒ Ⓓ Ⓔ
11. Ⓐ Ⓑ Ⓒ Ⓓ Ⓔ	23. Ⓐ Ⓑ Ⓒ Ⓓ Ⓔ	35. Ⓐ Ⓑ Ⓒ Ⓓ Ⓔ	47. Ⓐ Ⓑ Ⓒ Ⓓ Ⓔ	59. Ⓐ Ⓑ Ⓒ Ⓓ Ⓔ
12. Ⓐ Ⓑ Ⓒ Ⓓ Ⓔ	24. Ⓐ Ⓑ Ⓒ Ⓓ Ⓔ	36. Ⓐ Ⓑ Ⓒ Ⓓ Ⓔ	48. Ⓐ Ⓑ Ⓒ Ⓓ Ⓔ	60. Ⓐ Ⓑ Ⓒ Ⓓ Ⓔ

SECTION 4

1. Ⓐ Ⓑ Ⓒ Ⓓ Ⓔ	6. Ⓐ Ⓑ Ⓒ Ⓓ Ⓔ	11. Ⓐ Ⓑ Ⓒ Ⓓ Ⓔ	16. Ⓐ Ⓑ Ⓒ Ⓓ Ⓔ	21. Ⓐ Ⓑ Ⓒ Ⓓ Ⓔ
2. Ⓐ Ⓑ Ⓒ Ⓓ Ⓔ	7. Ⓐ Ⓑ Ⓒ Ⓓ Ⓔ	12. Ⓐ Ⓑ Ⓒ Ⓓ Ⓔ	17. Ⓐ Ⓑ Ⓒ Ⓓ Ⓔ	22. Ⓐ Ⓑ Ⓒ Ⓓ Ⓔ
3. Ⓐ Ⓑ Ⓒ Ⓓ Ⓔ	8. Ⓐ Ⓑ Ⓒ Ⓓ Ⓔ	13. Ⓐ Ⓑ Ⓒ Ⓓ Ⓔ	18. Ⓐ Ⓑ Ⓒ Ⓓ Ⓔ	23. Ⓐ Ⓑ Ⓒ Ⓓ Ⓔ
4. Ⓐ Ⓑ Ⓒ Ⓓ Ⓔ	9. Ⓐ Ⓑ Ⓒ Ⓓ Ⓔ	14. Ⓐ Ⓑ Ⓒ Ⓓ Ⓔ	19. Ⓐ Ⓑ Ⓒ Ⓓ Ⓔ	24. Ⓐ Ⓑ Ⓒ Ⓓ Ⓔ
5. Ⓐ Ⓑ Ⓒ Ⓓ Ⓔ	10. Ⓐ Ⓑ Ⓒ Ⓓ Ⓔ	15. Ⓐ Ⓑ Ⓒ Ⓓ Ⓔ	20. Ⓐ Ⓑ Ⓒ Ⓓ Ⓔ	25. Ⓐ Ⓑ Ⓒ Ⓓ Ⓔ

Writing Sample

Schools would like to get to know you better through a story you tell using one of the ideas below. Please choose the idea you find most interesting and write a story using the idea as your first sentence. Please fill in the circle next to the one you choose.

(A) What do you consider the three most important qualities of a good parent?

(B) They had never seen anything like it.

Use this page and the next page to complete your writing sample.

Continue on next page

SECTION 1
25 Questions

Following each problem in this section, there are five suggested answers. Work out each problem in your head or in the blank space provided at the right of the page. Then look at the five suggested answers and decide which one is best.

Note: Figures that accompany problems in this section are drawn as accurately as possible EXCEPT when it is stated in a specific problem that its figure is not drawn to scale.

Sample problem:

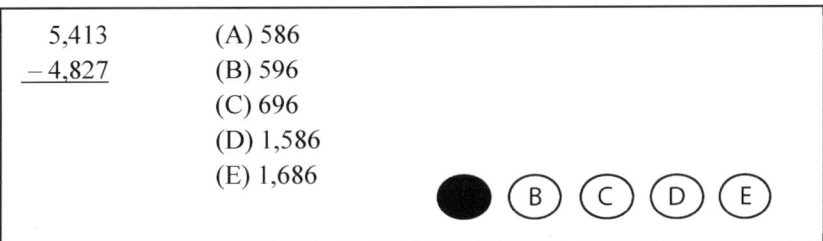

USE THIS SPACE FOR FIGURING.

1. There are 7 members in Peter's club. Peter currently has 10 cookies. If Peter wants to give 2 cookies to each member of his club, how many more cookies does he need to buy?

    (A) 2
    (B) 4
    (C) 6
    (D) 8
    (E) 9

2. Of the following, 3,567 divided by 41 is closest to

    (A) 10
    (B) 80
    (C) 90
    (D) 180
    (E) 900

GO ON TO THE NEXT PAGE.

Practice Test 4: Upper Level

USE THIS SPACE FOR FIGURING.

3. Ashley has 21 pencils and Troy has 3. How many pencils must Ashley give Troy if each is to have the same number?

   (A) 9
   (B) 18
   (C) 21
   (D) 24
   (E) It cannot be determined from the information given.

---

4. Mike has $x - 1$ notebooks. Jeff has two times the number of notebooks that Mike has. In terms of x, how many notebooks does Jeff have?

   (A) $2x - 1$
   (B) $x - 2$
   (C) $x - 3$
   (D) $2x - 2$
   (E) $2x - 4$

---

5. $0.30 \times 1.8 =$

   (A) 0.054
   (B) 0.54
   (C) 1.08
   (D) 5.4
   (E) 54

---

6. $1\frac{1}{4} + 2\frac{1}{8} + 3\frac{1}{16} =$

   (A) $6\frac{1}{16}$
   (B) $6\frac{7}{16}$
   (C) $7\frac{1}{4}$
   (D) $7\frac{6}{16}$
   (E) $13\frac{1}{16}$

GO ON TO THE NEXT PAGE.

USE THIS SPACE FOR FIGURING.

7. If $\frac{1}{4} + x > 1$, then x could be

   (A) $1/8$
   (B) $8/16$
   (C) $3/4$
   (D) $6/8$
   (E) $3/3$

8. Donna is 5 ft. 7 in. tall. Rachel is 3 in. shorter than Donna. If Elaina is 8 in. taller than Rachel, how tall is Elaina?

   (A) 5 ft. 6in.
   (B) 5 ft. 8 in.
   (C) 5 ft. 11 in.
   (D) 5 ft. 13 in.
   (E) 6 ft. 0 in.

9. If $3/6x = 21$, then $1/3x =$

   (A) 14
   (B) 18
   (C) 21
   (D) 36
   (E) 42

10. If 36 percent of b is 58, what is 18 percent of $2b$?

    (A) 29
    (B) 58
    (C) 116
    (D) 161
    (E) 322

GO ON TO THE NEXT PAGE.

USE THIS SPACE FOR FIGURING.

11. A studio is covering a 4 meter by 8 meter wall with wallpaper. If the total cost of the wallpaper used is $104, how much does the wallpaper cost per square meter?

    (A) $3.15
    (B) $3.17
    (C) $3.20
    (D) $3.23
    (E) $3.25

12. If $z + 3$ is an odd number, z could be equal to

    (A) 1
    (B) 3
    (C) 5
    (D) 21
    (E) 22

13. If the sum of 4 consecutive even numbers is 60, the largest of these numbers is

    (A) 14
    (B) 16
    (C) 18
    (D) 20
    (E) 22

14. If $N < 4$, which of the following CANNOT be a possible value of $3 - 2N$?

    (A) −6
    (B) −3
    (C) 0
    (D) 3
    (E) 6

GO ON TO THE NEXT PAGE.

15. Over the course of her life, Sophia wrote 36 novels. If she wrote 9 novels before she was 30 years old, what percentage of her novels did she write when she was 30 years or older?

    (A) 25%
    (B) 30%
    (C) 40%
    (D) 60%
    (E) 75%

16. In Figure 1, a square with a side length of 17 is adjacent to a square with a side length of 26. If the line segment where the two squares intersect has a length of 10, what is the perimeter of the whole figure?

    (A) 152
    (B) 154
    (C) 162
    (D) 164
    (E) 172

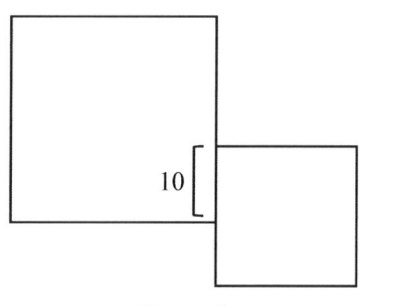

Figure 1

17. For what price is 30% off equal to $45 off?

    (A) $120
    (B) $130
    (C) $140
    (D) $150
    (E) $160

18. According to Figure 2, which of the following statements is/are correct?

   I. There are 5 more Fantasy books than Fiction books.
   II. There are more than twice as many Sci-Fi books as there are Horror books
   III. There are more Sci-Fi books than there are Fiction and Fantasy books combined.

   (A) I only
   (B) II only
   (C) I and II only
   (D) II and III only
   (E) I, II, and III

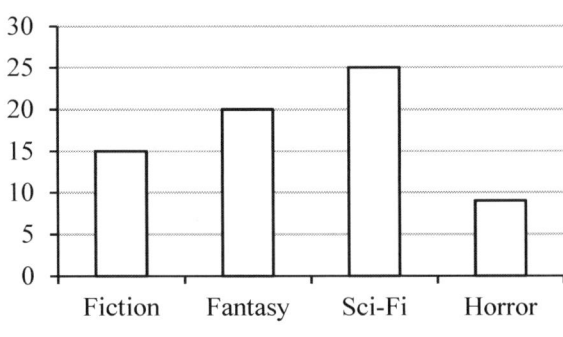

Figure 2

19. In Figure 3, a square has a diagonal whose length is 14. What is the area of the square?

   (A) 25
   (B) 49
   (C) 50
   (D) 98
   (E) 100

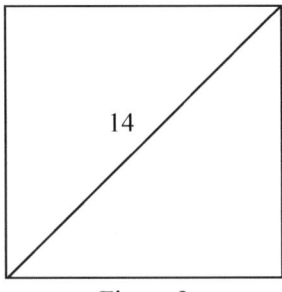

Figure 3

20. Joe's investment this year is worth $15,000, a 20% increase from last year's investment. What was Joe's investment worth last year?

   (A) $12,500
   (B) $12,750
   (C) $13,000
   (D) $14,980
   (E) $17,500

GO ON TO THE NEXT PAGE.

USE THIS SPACE FOR FIGURING.

21. In Figure 4, the letters A, B, and C each represent a unique non-zero integer. What is the value of C?

(A) 1

(B) 4

(C) 5

(D) 6

(E) 8

$$\begin{array}{r} BBA \\ +\ C1A \\ \hline 566 \end{array}$$

Figure 4

---

22. In a school of 100 students, students are enrolled in Spanish, French, or both Spanish and French classes. 45 students only take Spanish, and 19 students take both Spanish and French. How many total students take French?

(A) 9

(B) 36

(C) 55

(D) 64

(E) 81

---

23. A number is increased by 12% and then decreased by 24%. The result is approximately what percent of the original number?

(A) 12%

(B) 15%

(C) 24%

(D) 85%

(E) 115%

---

24. 3.654 is closest in value to

(A) 3.564

(B) 3.645

(C) 4.456

(D) 6.354

(E) 6.534

GO ON TO THE NEXT PAGE.

25. The length of a rectangle is three times its width. If the length and width are integer values, what could be the value of the rectangle's perimeter?

   (A) 9
   (B) 18
   (C) 25
   (D) 36
   (E) 64

STOP

IF YOU FINISH BEFORE TIME IS CALLED,
YOU MAY CHECK YOUR WORK ON THIS SECTION ONLY.
DO NOT TURN TO ANY OTHER SECTION IN THE TEST.

SECTION 2
40 Questions

Read each passage carefully and then answer the questions about it. For each question, decide on the basis of the passage which one of the choices best answers the question.

The Paleozoic ocean was dominated by animals known as nautiloids. These marine cephalopods were the main predators of the period, and were characterized by a tough external shell. In many species, the shell served not only as a form of protection, but also as a form of buoyancy control. The modern nautilus, for example—one of few surviving nautiloids—has a shell containing air-filled pockets, which
Line 5 help it to maintain neutral buoyancy in water.

Many modern cephalopods lack an external shell, but the shell usually isn't completely absent. Instead, modern cephalopods often possess an internal shell. In cuttlefish this shell is called the cuttlebone and, like the shell of the nautilus, contains gas filled pockets which help the cuttlefish to maintain buoyancy.

---

1. In this passage, the author's main purpose is to
   (A) entertain
   (B) speculate
   (C) inform
   (D) inquire
   (E) debunk

2. Nautilus shells contain gas-filled pockets
   (A) for the storage of food
   (B) for buoyancy control
   (C) to eliminate waste
   (D) to capture prey
   (E) for protection from predators

3. Based on the context of the passage, a "cephalopod" (line 6) most likely refers to
   (A) any animal with a shell
   (B) any marine predator
   (C) a type of Nautilus
   (D) an ancient nautiloid
   (E) a type of animal that includes the Nautiloids

4. What would be the best title for this passage?
   (A) The Shells of Nautiloids and Other Cephalopods
   (B) How Nautiloids Swim
   (C) The Difference Between a Cuttlefish and a Nautilus
   (D) Predators of The Ancient Ocean
   (E) Nautiloids: Living Fossils

GO ON TO THE NEXT PAGE.

5. It can be inferred from the passage that most nautiloids

    (A) possessed internal shells
    (B) hunted other nautiloids
    (C) are now extinct
    (D) could not swim
    (E) lacked external shells

A long time ago, when the world was much younger than it is now, people told and believed a great many wonderful stories about wonderful things which neither you nor I have ever seen. They often talked about a certain Mighty Being called Jupiter, or Zeus, who was king of the sky and the earth; and they said that he sat most of the time amid the clouds on the top of a very high mountain where he could
Line 5   look down and see everything that was going on in the earth beneath. He liked to ride on the storm-clouds and hurl burning thunderbolts right and left among the trees and rocks; and he was so very, very mighty that when he nodded, the earth quaked, the mountains trembled and smoked, the sky grew black, and the sun hid his face.

Jupiter had two brothers, both of them terrible fellows, but not nearly so great as himself. The
10   name of one of them was Neptune, or Poseidon, and he was the king of the sea. He had a glittering, golden palace far down in the deep sea-caves where the fishes live and the red coral grows; and whenever he was angry the waves would rise mountain high, and the storm-winds would howl fearfully, and the sea would try to break over the land; and men called him the Shaker of the Earth.

The other brother of Jupiter was a sad pale-faced being, whose kingdom was underneath the earth,
15   where the sun never shone and where there was darkness and weeping and sorrow all the time. His name was Pluto, or Aidoneus, and his country was called the Lower World, or the Land of Shadows, or Hades. Men said that whenever anyone died, Pluto would send his messenger, or Shadow Leader, to carry that one down into his cheerless kingdom; and for that reason they never spoke well of him, but thought of him only as the enemy of life.

6. What would be the best title for this passage?

(A) Weather Gods of the Ancient World
(B) How Gods are Made
(C) How the Planets Got Their Names
(D) The Origin of Hades
(E) Zeus and His Brothers

7. According to the passage, Neptune lived in

(A) undersea caverns
(B) the heavens
(C) a floating palace
(D) a storm cloud
(E) a mountain-high wave

8. The author's description of Pluto suggests that

(A) he was Jupiter's fiercest enemy
(B) he could control fire
(C) he could be harmed by sunlight
(D) he was evil and deceitful
(E) he was the king of the dead

GO ON TO THE NEXT PAGE.

9. Which of the following statements is implied by the passage?

   (A) People once used myths to frighten children.
   (B) People once controlled the weather by worshipping certain gods.
   (C) People once used myths to help navigate the oceans.
   (D) People once used myths as a way to explain natural events.
   (E) People once used myths to impart morals and discourage criminal behavior.

GO ON TO THE NEXT PAGE.

In a settlement called Pormpuraaw, on the northern tip of the Cape York Peninsula in Queensland, Australia, live a people called the Thaayorre. The Thaayorre speak a language called Kuuk Thaayorre, which shares several important features with other aboriginal languages: it is spoken by only a few hundred people (two hundred and fifty, at the last count); most of the dialects have been lost as the number of speakers has dwindled; and, in Kuuk Thaayorre, there is no word for "left" or "right." In fact, in Kuuk Thaayorre there is no subjective direction at all. All sixteen words for direction relate to the cardinal directions: North, East, South and West.

Kuuk Thaayorre uses cardinal directions instead of subjective direction at all scales, large and small. If you were speaking Kuuk Thaayorre, not only might you have to say something familiar like "you must walk north to reach the store," you might also have to say something like "your southeastern shoe is untied." If you lost track of your position relative to the cardinal directions, then you wouldn't be able to communicate effectively.

Owing to this peculiarity of their language, the Thaayorre people must always know which direction they are facing, even when they are inside or in unfamiliar surroundings. Fortunately, as recent research demonstrates, the Thaayorre and other people who speak similar languages have a special talent for that. They're even better at tracking their orientation than scientists had previously thought was possible.

Their abilities raise questions about the power of the human mind to achieve what was once thought impossible, and about the relationship between language and thought processes.

10. What does the author mean by "subjective direction" (line 6)?

(A) directions fixed to points in the world
(B) directions unique to aboriginal languages
(C) directions that rely on descriptions of landmarks
(D) directions that would be different from a different perspective
(E) directions that apply only to large objects

11. The author would most likely agree with which of the following statements about the Thaayorre people?

(A) They are very primitive.
(B) They cannot communicate effectively.
(C) They think more objectively than most other people.
(D) Their culture will soon be extinct.
(E) Their language and abilities raise questions about human potential.

GO ON TO THE NEXT PAGE.

12. The author implies that English speakers, unlike the Kuuk Thayyorre, normally use cardinal directions only

    (A) on large scales, for things that are big or far away
    (B) when they are inside
    (C) on small scales, for things that are small or nearby
    (D) when they cannot tell which way they are facing
    (E) when they are in familiar places

13. We can infer from the passage that

    (A) other aboriginal languages also rely on cardinal directions
    (B) scientists don't understand how we track subjective directions
    (C) cardinal directions are better than subjective directions
    (D) English has no words for cardinal directions
    (E) only the Thaayorre can speak Kuuk Thaayorre

GO ON TO THE NEXT PAGE.

Salt is often used as a de-icing agent on roads and sidewalks because a solution of salt and water has a lower freezing point than pure water. The ice exchanges molecules with the salt, creating a solution, and because this solution has a lower freezing point than pure water the ice usually melts. If the temperature is very cold, however, the ice may remain solid. In such cases, sand is spread over the

Line 5 surface of the ice in order to maintain traction, rather than trying to melt the ice.

Salt is also added to ice to make cold brine. The chemical reaction that occurs as the salt melts the ice actually reduces the temperature of the solution, resulting in liquid water which is colder than the normal freezing point of water. This effect is used when making ice cream: a container of flavored cream is frozen by submerging it in cold brine while stirring, although care is taken to avoid letting the

10 brine mix with the cream.

It is widely believed that salt also lowers the boiling point of water, but actually the opposite is true. Adding salt to water increases its boiling point, but it is a very small effect. Almost twelve teaspoons of salt would be required to increase the boiling point of an ounce of water by one degree Fahrenheit. However, while salt slightly increases the boiling point of water, it also causes it to heat

15 more rapidly. Therefore, the addition of salt can cause water to boil faster than it would without salt.

14. People often spread salt on icy streets and sidewalks in order to

    (A) generate heat that will melt the ice
    (B) increase traction
    (C) melt the ice by lowering its freezing point
    (D) warn drivers of icy conditions
    (E) make ice cream

15. Adding salt to water might cause it to boil sooner because

    (A) salt lowers the boiling point
    (B) the water will heat more quickly
    (C) salt increases the boiling point
    (D) adding salt to water generates heat
    (E) salt melts ice

16. According to the passage, what is "brine" (line 6)?

    (A) a solution of salt and water
    (B) frozen saltwater
    (C) boiling saltwater
    (D) a solution of sand and ice
    (E) an ingredient in ice cream

17. The author's style in this passage could best be described as

    (A) argumentative
    (B) expository
    (C) narrative
    (D) inquisitive
    (E) condescending

GO ON TO THE NEXT PAGE.

18. What would be the best title for this passage?

   (A) How to Make Ice Cream
   (B) Boiling with Salt: Fact or Fiction?
   (C) Road Safety in Icy Conditions
   (D) The Many Uses of Salt
   (E) A Brief History of Salt

GO ON TO THE NEXT PAGE.

Then consider this startling situation: Arsene Lupin was wandering about within the limited bounds of a transatlantic steamer; in that very small corner of the world, in that dining saloon, in that smoking room, in that music room! Arsene Lupin was, perhaps, this gentleman… or that one… my neighbor at the table… the sharer of my stateroom…

Line 5 "And this condition of affairs will last for five days!" exclaimed Miss Nelly Underdown, next morning. "It is unbearable! I hope he will be arrested."

Then, addressing me, she added:

"And you, Monsieur d'Andrezy, you are on intimate terms with the captain; surely you know something?"

19. The passage implies that Arsene Lupin

   (A) is a salesman
   (B) knows the ship's captain
   (C) has been arrested
   (D) is a criminal
   (E) is a friend of Monsieur d'Andrezy

20. Who is the narrator of this passage?

   (A) Nelly Underdown
   (B) Monsieur d'Andrezy
   (C) Arsene Lupin
   (D) the ship's captain
   (E) an unnamed person

21. When the narrator describes the "limited bounds of a transatlantic steamer" (lines 1-2), he or she is suggesting that

   (A) the steamer is a relatively small space
   (B) the steamer travels slowly
   (C) steamers are dangerous vehicles
   (D) the steamer is very crowded
   (E) the steamer's trip has a limited duration

22. The tone of the first paragraph creates a sense of

   (A) suspense
   (B) serenity
   (C) hopelessness
   (D) anger
   (E) disgust

23. Based on the description in the passage, Nelly Underdown would be best described as

   (A) forlorn
   (B) secretive
   (C) anxious
   (D) depressed
   (E) sea-sick

GO ON TO THE NEXT PAGE.

Chinese environmental officials are now raising the same concern that has worried environmental activists for years: that severe pollution has led to a rise of so-called "cancer villages." Activists and some journalists have been using the term "cancer villages" for several years to describe villages located close to waterways or industrial parks where cancer rates are very high.

Line 5 A report issued this week by China's Environment Ministry specifically mentions "cancer villages," blaming the problem on severe water and air pollution. It is thought to be one of the first times the term has been used by government officials. Official statistics indicate China has about 1,700 water pollution accidents each year and that up to 40 percent of the country's rivers are seriously polluted.

10 Water researcher Zhao Feihong at the Beijing Healthcare Association said last month that of the more than 100 rivers in Beijing only two or three can be used for tap water. "The rest of the rivers, if they have not dried up, then they are polluted by discharge," she said.

During the last week of January, smog hung over cities and towns from Liaoning in the north to as far south as Guangdong and air pollution reached unhealthy levels for long periods of time. Chinese *15* officials blamed industrial activity, construction and the widespread use of coal for heat.

24. It can be inferred from the passage that heavy pollution

    (A) occurs mainly around small villages
    (B) causes an increase in cancer rates
    (C) is only a problem in China
    (D) increases the demand for heating coal
    (E) mainly ends up in rivers

25. The passage was most likely taken from

    (A) a novel
    (B) a newspaper
    (C) an encyclopedia
    (D) a diary
    (E) a letter

26. Which of the following is NOT cited as a possible cause for high rates of cancer in "cancer villages?"

    (A) construction
    (B) water pollution
    (C) coal heating
    (D) food contamination
    (E) air pollution

27. What would the author most likely discuss next?

    (A) other risk factors for cancer
    (B) Chinese traditional medicine
    (C) the various ministries in the Chinese government
    (D) why some rivers can't be used for tap water
    (E) possible solutions for the problem of "cancer villages"

GO ON TO THE NEXT PAGE.

In a survey of American Institutions, there seem to be three fundamental principles on which they are based: first, that all people are naturally equal in rights; second, that a people cannot be taxed without their own consent; and third, that they may delegate their power of self-government to representatives chosen by themselves.

Line 5
The remote origin of these principles it is difficult to trace. Some suppose that they are innate, appealing to consciousness—concerning which there can be no dispute or argument. Others suppose that they exist only so far as people can assert and use them, whether granted by rulers or seized by society. Some find that they arose among ancient Teutonic peoples in their German forests, while still others go back to Jewish, Grecian, and Roman history for their origin. Wherever they originated, their

10
practical enforcement has been a slow and unequal growth among various peoples, and it is always the evident result of a process of gradual change through time.

28. The author asserts that the values of American institutions

(A) are unique to the United States
(B) are guaranteed in all democracies
(C) are the same values as those of ancient Rome
(D) are the result of a long process of development
(E) are impossible to enforce

29. According to the passage, some people believe that the fundamental principles of American institutions first appear

(A) in the struggle against Britain
(B) at the Boston Tea Party
(C) in ancient Greek, Jewish, and Roman civilizations
(D) in the Constitution
(E) in the delegation of powers

30. Which motto best summarizes the second and third principles in lines 2-4?

(A) No Taxation Without Representation
(B) With Liberty and Justice for All
(C) From Many, One
(D) United We Stand, Divided We Fall
(E) Equality Before the Law

31. What does the author mean when he states that principles "exist only so far as people can assert and use them" (line 7)?

(A) Nobody actually has any principles.
(B) Rights only exist if they can be exercised
(C) You don't deserve something unless you can take it by force.
(D) People only have rights if they have a constitution.
(E) Animals do not have any rights.

32. The author's intention is to

(A) discuss the principles upon which American institutions are based
(B) persuade the reader of the correctness of American principles
(C) determine what makes American principles different from those of other nations
(D) criticize America's founding principles
(E) dispute false theories about American history

GO ON TO THE NEXT PAGE.

We stood together at the top of the cliff, in a dry and gentle breeze. A hawk hovered in the distance, riding the thermals. In that vast expanse, the only sound was the wind. We spoke in whispers, and she said "It's so quiet."

"I know" came my reply. Somehow those words didn't seem like enough, and I added "I bet if I shouted, it would echo for miles."

Turning to me, she asked "Why don't you?"

I thought about it. Why not? There's nothing hard about shouting. It seemed like it could be fun. But although I am ashamed to admit it, the keenest consideration was that it seemed as though I had been challenged. With my masculinity at stake I resolved to let out a manly shout and to make the canyon echo with my voice; but as I took a breath, something restrained me.

There was a sacred quality in the vast depth of the silence, and it affected me. An aversion to blasphemy welled up inside me, and I could not compel myself to shatter the peace of the moment. I exhaled quietly, and as my breath mingled with the passing breeze I confessed "I don't think I can. It seems wrong."

"I know" she said, and we stood there a while longer without speaking. Eventually, we left the silence of the cliff and headed back to the trail; but the silence never left me—not entirely. In a peaceful moment, I can still hear it—and I still can't bring myself to break it.

33. Why did the narrator refrain from shouting?

    (A) He suddenly felt short of breath.
    (B) He didn't want to violate the sanctity of a peaceful moment.
    (C) He was embarrassed to think that someone might hear him.
    (D) He thought that it would be disgraceful to shout just because of a challenge.
    (E) He was concerned that he might frighten the hawk.

34. Based on the context of the passage, "riding the thermals" (line 2) probably means that the hawk was

    (A) flapping its wings
    (B) hunting its prey
    (C) diving from the sky
    (D) calling to its mate
    (E) gliding on the wind

35. What does the narrator mean when he says "the silence never left me" (line 16)?

    (A) He was struck deaf.
    (B) He is able to ignore loud noises by remembering the silence.
    (C) He is still affected by the memory of the silence.
    (D) He is now attracted to quiet places.
    (E) The only thing he remembers about that day is the silence.

36. What best describes the narrator's attitude towards the silence of the cliff?

    (A) reverent
    (B) defiant
    (C) resentful
    (D) submissive
    (E) confused

GO ON TO THE NEXT PAGE.

> I met a traveller from an antique land
> Who said: Two vast and trunkless legs of stone
> Stand in the desert. Near them on the sand,
> Half sunk, a shatter'd visage lies, whose frown
> Line 5   And wrinkled lip and sneer of cold command
> Tell that its sculptor well those passions read
> Which yet survive, stamp'd on these lifeless things,
> The hand that mock'd them and the heart that fed.
> And on the pedestal these words appear:
> 10   "My name is Ozymandias, king of kings:
> Look on my works, ye Mighty, and despair!"
> Nothing beside remains: round the decay
> Of that colossal wreck, boundless and bare,
> The lone and level sands stretch far away.

37. What does the inscription in lines 10-11 suggest about Ozymandias?

    (A) He knew that the statue would be the only thing left standing in that place.
    (B) He hated other kings.
    (C) He didn't want to build any more statues.
    (D) He thought that his works exceeded all others.
    (E) He was a kind and humble king.

38. What best describes the main message of this poem?

    (A) Only love lasts forever.
    (B) Stories can travel around the world.
    (C) Even mighty empires succumb to time.
    (D) Ozymandias was the greatest king.
    (E) Sand eventually covers everything.

39. What best describes the tone of this poem?

    (A) hateful
    (B) disingenuous
    (C) nostalgic
    (D) humorous
    (E) somber

40. The poem is written from the perspective of

    (A) a traveler in a foreign land
    (B) someone who is retelling a story
    (C) Ozymandias, King of Kings
    (D) a sculptor whose work is now ruined
    (E) someone who has discovered an ancient statue

STOP

IF YOU FINISH BEFORE TIME IS CALLED,
YOU MAY CHECK YOUR WORK ON THIS SECTION ONLY.
DO NOT TURN TO ANY OTHER SECTION IN THE TEST.

SECTION 3
60 Questions

This section consists of two different types of questions: synonyms and analogies. There are directions and a sample question for each type.

Synonyms

Each of the following questions consists of one word followed by five words or phrases. You are to select the one word or phrase whose meaning is closest to the word in capital letters.

Sample Question:

CHILLY:
(A) lazy
(B) nice
(C) dry
(D) cold
(E) sunny

Ⓐ Ⓑ Ⓒ ● Ⓔ

---

1. ILLICIT:
   (A) evil
   (B) untidy
   (C) prohibited
   (D) exaggerated
   (E) sultry

2. SOW:
   (A) stitch
   (B) pig
   (C) canal
   (D) till
   (E) irrigate

3. JEER:
   (A) praise
   (B) annoy
   (C) activate
   (D) mock
   (E) shake

4. KEEN:
   (A) sharp
   (B) indignant
   (C) wicked
   (D) above
   (E) askew

5. MIRTH:
   (A) gift
   (B) depression
   (C) clarity
   (D) gold
   (E) amusement

6. LINGER:
   (A) revert
   (B) delay
   (C) hurry
   (D) remark
   (E) ache

GO ON TO THE NEXT PAGE.

7. ADMIRE:
   (A) impugn
   (B) sing
   (C) count
   (D) adopt
   (E) respect

8. PERSECUTE:
   (A) assume
   (B) invade
   (C) govern
   (D) oppress
   (E) convict

9. APPREHENSIVE:
   (A) doubtful
   (B) captive
   (C) tidy
   (D) lost
   (E) just

10. COUNSEL:
    (A) letter
    (B) monitor
    (C) advice
    (D) carelessness
    (E) meeting

11. COMPOSURE:
    (A) self-control
    (B) author
    (C) preface
    (D) midpoint
    (E) conductor

12. IMMACULATE:
    (A) shackled
    (B) warranted
    (C) flawless
    (D) indigo
    (E) messy

13. TURBULENT:
    (A) breathless
    (B) drizzly
    (C) obnoxious
    (D) arrogant
    (E) disordered

14. LADEN:
    (A) burdened
    (B) upheld
    (C) submerged
    (D) broken
    (E) unjust

15. IMPEDE:
    (A) increase
    (B) ply
    (C) prepare
    (D) sail
    (E) block

16. EXPEDITE:
    (A) construct
    (B) incite
    (C) record
    (D) hurry
    (E) dabble

GO ON TO THE NEXT PAGE.

17. CONTAMINATE:
    (A) destroy
    (B) pollute
    (C) exhaust
    (D) merge
    (E) consume

18. PARRY:
    (A) deflect
    (B) abridge
    (C) collect
    (D) exhale
    (E) prohibit

19. NOTORIOUS:
    (A) infamous
    (B) masculine
    (C) gelatinous
    (D) numerous
    (E) regular

20. EXUBERANT:
    (A) magical
    (B) slippery
    (C) exhausted
    (D) enthusiastic
    (E) implied

21. ETERNAL:
    (A) ephemeral
    (B) internal
    (C) final
    (D) unending
    (E) outside

22. BOLSTER:
    (A) demolish
    (B) support
    (C) invite
    (D) lock
    (E) remake

23. EMACIATED:
    (A) eviscerated
    (B) ashen
    (C) thin
    (D) incarcerated
    (E) wilted

24. NIMBLE:
    (A) jumpy
    (B) agile
    (C) nervous
    (D) soon
    (E) runner

25. DIPLOMAT:
    (A) governor
    (B) representative
    (C) ally
    (D) nemesis
    (E) general

26. PLUMMET:
    (A) fall
    (B) indicate
    (C) celebrate
    (D) hasten
    (E) undermine

GO ON TO THE NEXT PAGE.

27. FRAUD:
    (A) deception
    (B) deterrent
    (C) propaganda
    (D) coercion
    (E) enforcer

28. MOLTEN:
    (A) shed
    (B) pursued
    (C) burnished
    (D) liquefied
    (E) glowing

29. SWINDLE:
    (A) open
    (B) invent
    (C) control
    (D) invert
    (E) cheat

30. INVISIBLE:
    (A) silent
    (B) unseen
    (C) buried
    (D) secure
    (E) unpredictable

GO ON TO THE NEXT PAGE.

Analogies

The following questions ask you to find relationships between words. For each question, select the answer choice that best completes the meaning of the sentence.

Sample Question:

> Kitten is to cat as
> (A) fawn is to colt
> (B) puppy is to dog
> (C) cow is to bull
> (D) wolf is to bear
> (E) hen is to rooster
>
>

Choice (B) is the best answer because a kitten is a young cat just as a puppy is a young dog. Of all the answer choices, (B) states a relationship that is most like the relationship between kitten and cat.

---

31. Grapes are to wine as

    (A) bread is to toast
    (B) tomato is to salad
    (C) milk is to cheese
    (D) happiness is to song
    (E) melons are to seeds

32. Tailor is to clothing as

    (A) nanny is to children
    (B) cobbler is to shoes
    (C) miller is to grain
    (D) banker is to business
    (E) officer is to army

33. Subtle is to obvious as

    (A) shadow is to pale
    (B) inferred is to implied
    (C) meek is to timid
    (D) bright is to sunny
    (E) quiet is to loud

34. Bat is to racket as

    (A) baseball is to tennis ball
    (B) game is to player
    (C) soccer is to kickball
    (D) basketball is to net
    (E) goalie is to hockey

35. Ambassador is to diplomacy as

    (A) president is to nation
    (B) clerk is to documents
    (C) spy is to espionage
    (D) covert is to hidden
    (E) initiate is to veteran

36. Actor is to theater as

    (A) audience is to speech
    (B) singer is to music
    (C) painter is to easel
    (D) hangar is to aircraft
    (E) lawyer is to courtroom

GO ON TO THE NEXT PAGE.

37. Sweet is to savory as
    (A) taste is to sour
    (B) color is to red
    (C) sugar is to salt
    (D) flavor is to odor
    (E) dessert is to enjoy

38. Refute is to argument as
    (A) debunk is to myth
    (B) quarrel is to sibling
    (C) concede is to debate
    (D) descend is to precipice
    (E) compete is to opponent

39. Water is to pipe as
    (A) ocean is to sea
    (B) liquid is to jug
    (C) electricity is to wire
    (D) driver is to car
    (E) cloud is to storm

40. Annoyed is to distraught as
    (A) visited is to deported
    (B) guilty is to convicted
    (C) moody is to depressed
    (D) amused is to pleased
    (E) arrested is to detained

41. Indigenous is to native as foreign is to
    (A) commerce
    (B) domestic
    (C) unusual
    (D) government
    (E) alien

42. Antiseptic is to germs as
    (A) fertilizer is to plants
    (B) bandage is to wounds
    (C) bleach is to clothes
    (D) pesticide is to insects
    (E) kindling is to fires

43. Guts are to bravery as
    (A) hearts are to circulation
    (B) feet are to leg
    (C) wrists are to writing
    (D) lungs are to confidence
    (E) brains are to intelligence

44. Botched is to ineptly as perfect is to
    (A) expertly
    (B) implicitly
    (C) poorly
    (D) quickly
    (E) hardly

45. Principal is to school as
    (A) surgeon is to operation
    (B) farmer is to plow
    (C) foreman is to factory
    (D) author is to novel
    (E) policeman is to arrest

46. Vow is to promise as epiphany is to
    (A) oath
    (B) speech
    (C) confusion
    (D) silence
    (E) realization

GO ON TO THE NEXT PAGE.

47. Habit is to individual as
    (A) law is to judge
    (B) tradition is to practice
    (C) custom is to society
    (D) culture is to global
    (E) consensus is to group

48. Indifferent is to apathy as
    (A) placid is to vigor
    (B) provocation is to anger
    (C) suspicious is to trust
    (D) vexed is to anxiety
    (E) annoyed is to nuisance

49. Papyrus is to scroll as
    (A) vellum is to skin
    (B) clay is to tablet
    (C) percussion is to instrument
    (D) chapter is to book
    (E) feather is to bird

50. Cavernous is to hollow as calamitous is to
    (A) important
    (B) uneventful
    (C) unfortunate
    (D) typical
    (E) deep

51. Douse is to flame as
    (A) wreck is to car
    (B) rain is to weather
    (C) quash is to rebellion
    (D) lamp is to light
    (E) captivate is to audience

52. Jaywalker is to criminal as
    (A) prisoner is to warden
    (B) soil is to earth
    (C) collision is to injury
    (D) misdemeanor is to felony
    (E) legal is to illegal

53. Sated is to ravenous as quenched is to
    (A) parched
    (B) thirst
    (C) barren
    (D) hungry
    (E) appetite

54. Generous is to philanthropist as
    (A) unlikely is to outcome
    (B) stingy is to miser
    (C) merciless is to victim
    (D) wealthy is to accountant
    (E) virtuous is to philosopher

55. Transgress is to law as
    (A) commit is to crime
    (B) decide is to selection
    (C) ignore is to avoidance
    (D) study is to prepare
    (E) violate is to agreement

56. Jettison is to cargo as
    (A) deliver is to parcel
    (B) flotsam is to debris
    (C) immigrate is to nation
    (D) evict is to tenant
    (E) passenger is to ship

GO ON TO THE NEXT PAGE.

57. Saunter is to sprint as drizzle is to

(A) hail
(B) speed
(C) pour
(D) taste
(E) trickle

58. Botanist is to plants as

(A) economist is to newspaper
(B) geologist is to minerals
(C) impressionist is to people
(D) astronomer is to astronauts
(E) meteorologist is to forecasts

59. Prohibit is to allow as

(A) entice is to lure
(B) assume is to fact
(C) personal is to individual
(D) encourage is to dissuade
(E) disown is to forget

60. Evaporate is to condense as

(A) thaw is to freeze
(B) heat is to liquid
(C) boil is to dry
(D) snow is to rain
(E) water is to steam

STOP

IF YOU FINISH BEFORE TIME IS CALLED,
YOU MAY CHECK YOUR WORK ON THIS SECTION ONLY.
DO NOT TURN TO ANY OTHER SECTION IN THE TEST.

SECTION 4
25 Questions

Following each problem in this section, there are five suggested answers. Work out each problem in your head or in the blank space provided at the right of the page. Then look at the five suggested answers and decide which one is best.

Note: Figures that accompany problems in this section are drawn as accurately as possible EXCEPT when it is stated in a specific problem that its figure is not drawn to scale.

Sample problem:

5,413	(A) 586
−4,827	(B) 596
	(C) 696
	(D) 1,586
	(E) 1,686

● Ⓑ Ⓒ Ⓓ Ⓔ

USE THIS SPACE FOR FIGURING.

1. In Figure 1, the perimeter of the polygon is 60. If all the sides in the polygon are of equal length, what is the length of one side?

    (A) 12
    (B) 15
    (C) 16
    (D) 20
    (E) 60

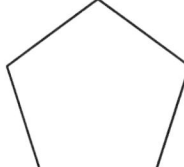

Figure 1

2. 13 divides evenly into which of the following numbers?

    (A) 141
    (B) 142
    (C) 143
    (D) 144
    (E) 145

GO ON TO THE NEXT PAGE.

3. $2\frac{4}{6} + 2\frac{2}{4} =$

   (A) $4\frac{4}{10}$

   (B) $4\frac{8}{10}$

   (C) $4\frac{6}{10}$

   (D) $5\frac{1}{6}$

   (E) $5\frac{10}{6}$

Questions 4-5 are based on the graph in Figure 2.

4. How many fewer waffles were sold on Friday than on Sunday?

   (A) 2
   (B) 20
   (C) 25
   (D) 2000
   (E) 3000

5. The number of waffles sold on Saturday is about how many times the number of waffles sold on Sunday?

   (A) 0.25
   (B) 0.75
   (C) 1.20
   (D) 1.80
   (E) 25

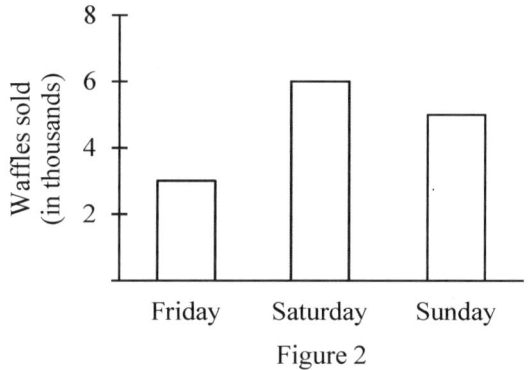

Figure 2

---

6. 1.961 is closest to

   (A) 1.691
   (B) 1.916
   (C) 1.963
   (D) 1.936
   (E) 2

7. The remainder when 57 is divided by 6 is equivalent to the remainder when 65 is divided by

   (A) 5
   (B) 15
   (C) 30
   (D) 31
   (E) 63

8. If $\frac{3}{2}x > 6$, then x could be

   (A) 1
   (B) 2
   (C) 3
   (D) 4
   (E) 5

9. On the number line in Figure 3, which letter represents the number 24?

   (A) A
   (B) B
   (C) C
   (D) D
   (E) None of the above.

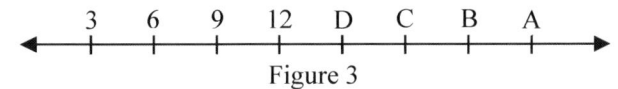

Figure 3

10. If 3 cartons weigh 16 pounds, what is the weight of 7.5 cartons?

    (A) 16 pounds
    (B) 32 pounds
    (C) 36 pounds
    (D) 40 pounds
    (E) 120 pounds

11. For any numbers p and s, $p \blacksquare s = p + 2s$.

    For example, $4 \blacksquare 5 = 4 + 2 \times 5 = 14$.

    Which expression best represents the value of $p \blacksquare 3$?

    (A) $p + 3$
    (B) $p + 6$
    (C) $p + 3s$
    (D) $p + 6s$
    (E) $2p + 3$

12. Jane lives 4 miles away from school. If Sasha lives 3 miles away from school, what is the distance between Jane's home and Sasha's home, in miles?

    (A) 1
    (B) 2
    (C) 4
    (D) 7
    (E) It cannot be determined from the information given.

13. A store has discounted all merchandise by 50%. One item is discounted an additional 10% off of this sale price. What is the total discount for this particular item?

    (A) 40% off
    (B) 45% off
    (C) 55% off
    (D) 60% off
    (E) 70% off

14. There are 6 officials waiting to ride in a limo. If there are 4 limos and at least one official must ride in each limo, what is the greatest number of officials who could ride in one limo?

    (A) 2
    (B) 3
    (C) 4
    (D) 5
    (E) 6

15. In Figure 4, what is the value of x?

    (A) 10
    (B) 20
    (C) 30
    (D) 40
    (E) 50

    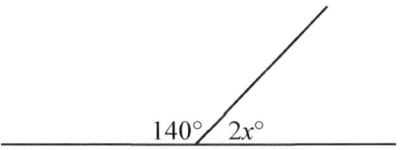

    Figure 4

16. A company has 3 full-time employees and 4 part-time employees. The full-time employees each work an average of 8 hours a day and the part-time employees each work an average of 4.5 hours a day. For all 7 employees, the average number of hours worked per day is

    (A) 5.5
    (B) 6
    (C) 6.5
    (D) 12.5
    (E) It cannot be determined from the information given.

17. If $2A + D = 6$ and $D + A = 3$, what is the value of D?

    (A) 0
    (B) 1
    (C) 2
    (D) 3
    (E) 6

18. A small cube has a side length of 3 inches. How many small cubes are needed to make a large cube with a side length of 12 inches?

    (A) 4
    (B) 16
    (C) 32
    (D) 64
    (E) 128

19. There are an equal number of motorcycles and cars in a garage. If the sum of the number of motorcycle wheels and car wheels equals 30, how many motorcycles are in the garage?

    (A) 3
    (B) 4
    (C) 5
    (D) 6
    (E) 15

20. Harvey's total commute is 1 hour and 30 minutes long. How long does it take Harvey to complete two-thirds of his commute?

    (A) 20 minutes
    (B) 30 minutes
    (C) 45 minutes
    (D) 50 minutes
    (E) 60 minutes

21. 20% of a is equal to b. What is 35% of b, in terms of a?

    (A) $0.07a$
    (B) $0.14a$
    (C) $0.15a$
    (D) $0.35a$
    (E) $0.70a$

GO ON TO THE NEXT PAGE.

22. If $a = \frac{2}{3}b$ and $c = \frac{1}{2}b$, c is equal to

   (A) $a/4$
   (B) $\frac{3a}{4}$
   (C) a
   (D) ab
   (E) $\frac{4a}{3}$

23. $4\overline{)733}$

   (A) $\frac{730}{4} + 3$
   (B) $\frac{700}{4} + 33$
   (C) $\frac{700 \times 30 \times 2}{4}$
   (D) $\frac{7}{4} + \frac{3}{4} + \frac{3}{4}$
   (E) $\frac{700}{4} + \frac{30}{4} + \frac{3}{4}$

24. If the average of four consecutive integers is 12.5, what is the second largest of these integers?

   (A) 11
   (B) 12
   (C) 12.5
   (D) 13
   (E) 14

25. The slope of a line that is parallel to $-3x + 2y = 5$ is

    (A) $-3/2$
    (B) $-2/3$
    (C) $2/5$
    (D) $2/3$
    (E) $3/2$

STOP
IF YOU FINISH BEFORE TIME IS CALLED,
YOU MAY CHECK YOUR WORK ON THIS SECTION ONLY.
DO NOT TURN TO ANY OTHER SECTION IN THE TEST.

Answers and Scoring
Chapter 4

Middle Level
Practice Test 1

Section 1 (Pages 37-44)

1. A	6. D	11. D	16. D	21. A
2. A	7. B	12. C	17. D	22. D
3. B	8. B	13. E	18. C	23. B
4. A	9. C	14. A	19. D	24. C
5. E	10. E	15. D	20. C	25. E

Section 2 (Pages 46-57)

1. C	9. A	17. A	25. C	33. D
2. D	10. C	18. D	26. E	34. E
3. A	11. B	19. B	27. C	35. A
4. E	12. E	20. A	28. B	36. C
5. B	13. B	21. E	29. A	37. E
6. A	14. E	22. B	30. D	38. A
7. E	15. C	23. D	31. D	39. B
8. D	16. D	24. D	32. C	40. B

Section 3 (Pages 58-65)

1. A	13. C	25. A	37. C	49. B
2. E	14. E	26. A	38. B	50. B
3. B	15. B	27. A	39. E	51. B
4. E	16. A	28. E	40. D	52. E
5. E	17. E	29. D	41. A	53. A
6. D	18. E	30. C	42. A	54. E
7. A	19. B	31. C	43. C	55. A
8. C	20. D	32. D	44. E	56. C
9. D	21. C	33. D	45. B	57. B
10. B	22. C	34. B	46. A	58. E
11. A	23. D	35. D	47. C	59. D
12. B	24. B	36. E	48. C	60. D

Section 4 (Pages 66-73)

1. D	6. E	11. D	16. B	21. C
2. C	7. D	12. E	17. A	22. B
3. D	8. B	13. D	18. C	23. A
4. A	9. A	14. C	19. B	24. A
5. D	10. C	15. B	20. A	25. E

Scoring Your Test

First, count up the number of questions you answered correctly, the number of questions you skipped, and the number of questions you answered incorrectly. Then, calculate your raw score using the following formula:

$$\text{Raw Score} = \text{\# of questions correct} - \frac{\text{\# of questions incorrect}}{4}$$

Add together your raw scores from your two math sections in order to determine your total raw math score.

Once you have found your raw score, convert it into an approximate scaled score using the estimated scoring charts on the next page. Keep in mind that you may score within 100 points of this estimate when you take your actual SSAT exam.

My Raw Score for Practice Test 1				
Section	# of Questions Correct	# of Questions Incorrect		Raw Score
Verbal	−	÷ 4	=	
Reading	−	÷ 4	=	
Math 1 + Math 2	−	÷ 4	=	

Scaled Score

Once you have found your raw score, convert it into an approximate **scaled score** using the scoring charts that follow. These charts provide an estimate for your SSAT scaled score based on your performance on this practice test. Keep in mind that your scaled score may differ within 100 points of this estimate when you take your actual SSAT exam, depending on the SSAT's specific scaling for that exam and any differences in your own test-taking process.

	Middle Level Scaled Scores		
Raw Score	Math	Reading	Verbal
60			710
55			710
50	710		710
45	680		700
40	660	710	675
35	635	685	650
30	615	655	625
25	590	625	600
20	570	595	580
15	540	565	555
10	525	535	530
5	500	505	505
0	480	475	480
-5	460	445	460
-10 and lower	440	440	440

Percentile

When you take your actual SSAT exam, you will also receive a **percentile** ranking comparing your performance against the performance of other students of your gender and grade who have taken the SSAT within the past three years. For example, a percentile of 62 means that you scored higher than 62% of other SSAT test-takers of your gender and grade. Because your percentile ranking shows how well you performed according to your own grade level, these rankings are frequently given the most consideration by admissions offices.

The following chart provides an estimate of your SSAT percentile ranking based on your **raw scores** for this practice test. Keep in mind that the percentiles below are estimates only and are not specific to your own grade and gender. Because younger students are expected to score differently than older students on this exam, your percentile may be higher or lower than this estimate depending on your grade.

Middle Level Percentiles			
Raw Score	Math	Reading	Verbal
60			99
55			99
50	99		97
45	93		93
40	80	99	85
35	65	96	75
30	50	82	62
25	36	63	47
20	23	43	31
15	13	24	18
10	6	11	8
5	2	3	2
0	1	1	1
-5	1	1	1
-10 and lower	1	1	1

Practice Test 1

The following chart shows the median (50th percentile) **scaled scores** for each grade level. If you are scoring at the median for your grade level, this means that you scored higher than half of your peers.

Middle Level Median Scores			
Grade	Math	Reading	Verbal
Grade 5	587	585	590
Grade 6	611	603	610
Grade 7	635	628	635

Middle Level
Practice Test 2

Section 1 (Pages 83-90)

1. D	6. A	11. D	16. B	21. D
2. D	7. C	12. C	17. B	22. E
3. E	8. D	13. D	18. B	23. E
4. E	9. D	14. C	19. B	24. C
5. B	10. E	15. A	20. D	25. A

Section 2 (Pages 92-105)

1. B	9. C	17. A	25. E	33. B
2. C	10. C	18. E	26. B	34. B
3. D	11. B	19. C	27. D	35. D
4. A	12. A	20. A	28. B	36. D
5. D	13. C	21. C	29. A	37. D
6. B	14. B	22. B	30. C	38. E
7. B	15. C	23. B	31. C	39. D
8. B	16. D	24. D	32. D	40. C

Section 3 (Pages 106-113)

1. B	13. C	25. B	37. B	49. A
2. C	14. E	26. A	38. C	50. B
3. E	15. C	27. C	39. E	51. A
4. D	16. B	28. B	40. A	52. C
5. B	17. B	29. C	41. D	53. C
6. A	18. C	30. A	42. C	54. D
7. B	19. C	31. D	43. B	55. E
8. D	20. E	32. B	44. C	56. D
9. A	21. C	33. E	45. B	57. A
10. C	22. D	34. A	46. A	58. E
11. E	23. B	35. D	47. D	59. A
12. A	24. D	36. C	48. E	60. B

Section 4 (Pages 114-122)

1. E	6. B	11. A	16. C	21. B
2. B	7. D	12. D	17. A	22. B
3. E	8. B	13. C	18. B	23. C
4. A	9. E	14. D	19. A	24. D
5. E	10. C	15. D	20. D	25. C

Scoring Your Test

First, count up the number of questions you answered correctly, the number of questions you skipped, and the number of questions you answered incorrectly. Then, calculate your raw score using the following formula:

$$\text{Raw Score} = \text{\# of questions correct} - \frac{\text{\# of questions incorrect}}{4}$$

Add together your raw scores from your two math sections in order to determine your total raw math score.

Once you have found your raw score, convert it into an approximate scaled score using the estimated scoring charts on the next page. Keep in mind that you may score within 100 points of this estimate when you take your actual SSAT exam.

	My Raw Score for Practice Test 2		
Section	# of Questions Correct	# of Questions Incorrect	Raw Score
Verbal	—	÷ 4	=
Reading	—	÷ 4	=
Math 1 + Math 2	—	÷ 4	=

Scaled Score

Once you have found your raw score, convert it into an approximate **scaled score** using the scoring charts that follow. These charts provide an estimate for your SSAT scaled score based on your performance on this practice test. Keep in mind that your scaled score may differ within 100 points of this estimate when you take your actual SSAT exam, depending on the SSAT's specific scaling for that exam and any differences in your own test-taking process.

Middle Level Scaled Scores			
Raw Score	Math	Reading	Verbal
60			710
55			710
50	710		710
45	680		700
40	660	710	675
35	635	685	650
30	615	655	625
25	590	625	600
20	570	595	580
15	540	565	555
10	525	535	530
5	500	505	505
0	480	475	480
-5	460	445	460
-10 and lower	440	440	440

Percentile

When you take your actual SSAT exam, you will also receive a percentile ranking comparing your performance against the performance of other students of your gender and grade who have taken the SSAT within the past three years. For example, a percentile of 62 means that you scored higher than 62% of other SSAT test-takers of your gender and grade. Because your percentile ranking shows how well you performed according to your own grade level, these rankings are frequently given the most consideration by admissions offices.

The following chart provides an estimate of your SSAT percentile ranking based on your **raw scores** for this practice test. Keep in mind that the percentiles below are estimates only and are not specific to your own grade and gender. Because younger students are expected to score differently than older students on this exam, your percentile may be higher or lower than this estimate depending on your grade.

Middle Level Percentiles			
Raw Score	Math	Reading	Verbal
60			99
55			99
50	99		97
45	93		93
40	80	99	85
35	65	96	75
30	50	82	62
25	36	63	47
20	23	43	31
15	13	24	18
10	6	11	8
5	2	3	2
0	1	1	1
-5	1	1	1
-10 and lower	1	1	1

The following chart shows the median (50th percentile) **scaled scores** for each grade level. If you are scoring at the median for your grade level, this means that you scored higher than half of your peers.

Middle Level Median Scores			
Grade	Math	Reading	Verbal
Grade 5	587	585	590
Grade 6	611	603	610
Grade 7	635	628	635

Upper Level
Practice Test 3

Section 1 (Pages 131-138)

1. A	6. C	11. C	16. E	21. E
2. D	7. C	12. B	17. B	22. C
3. D	8. A	13. B	18. D	23. E
4. B	9. C	14. E	19. E	24. A
5. B	10. D	15. A	20. E	25. B

Section 2 (Pages 140-154)

1. D	9. E	17. C	25. A	33. B
2. B	10. D	18. B	26. B	34. D
3. B	11. D	19. C	27. D	35. E
4. E	12. E	20. B	28. B	36. D
5. C	13. B	21. B	29. A	37. A
6. C	14. D	22. D	30. D	38. B
7. A	15. B	23. E	31. C	39. E
8. B	16. C	24. C	32. A	40. D

Section 3 (Pages 156-163)

1. C	13. D	25. C	37. B	49. A
2. E	14. E	26. A	38. C	50. D
3. B	15. D	27. A	39. A	51. A
4. B	16. C	28. C	40. B	52. C
5. E	17. C	29. E	41. E	53. E
6. B	18. A	30. D	42. B	54. D
7. A	19. D	31. C	43. B	55. B
8. C	20. A	32. B	44. E	56. C
9. D	21. D	33. E	45. B	57. E
10. C	22. A	34. D	46. D	58. A
11. D	23. B	35. C	47. D	59. C
12. B	24. E	36. A	48. B	60. A

Section 4 (Pages 164-171)

1. B	6. E	11. A	16. A	21. B
2. D	7. D	12. A	17. B	22. D
3. B	8. A	13. D	18. C	23. B
4. E	9. B	14. C	19. E	24. C
5. C	10. D	15. B	20. E	25. C

Scoring Your Test

First, count up the number of questions you answered correctly, the number of questions you skipped, and the number of questions you answered incorrectly. Then, calculate your raw score using the following formula:

$$\text{Raw Score} = \text{\# of questions correct} - \frac{\text{\# of questions incorrect}}{4}$$

Add together your raw scores from your two math sections in order to determine your total raw math score.

Once you have found your raw score, convert it into an approximate scaled score using the estimated scoring charts on the next page. Keep in mind that you may score within 100 points of this estimate when you take your actual SSAT exam.

My Raw Score for Practice Test 3				
Section	# of Questions Correct	# of Questions Incorrect		Raw Score
Verbal	—	÷ 4	=	
Reading	—	÷ 4	=	
Math 1 + Math 2	—	÷ 4	=	

Scaled Score

Once you have found your raw score, convert it into an approximate **scaled score** using the scoring charts that follow. These charts provide an estimate for your SSAT scaled score based on your performance on this practice test. Keep in mind that your scaled score may differ within 100 points of this estimate when you take your actual SSAT exam, depending on the SSAT's specific scaling for that exam and any differences in your own test-taking process.

Upper Level Scaled Scores			
Raw Score	Math	Reading	Verbal
60			800
55			800
50	800		780
45	780		750
40	755	800	725
35	725	720	700
30	700	690	645
25	670	660	645
20	640	630	615
15	615	600	590
10	585	570	565
5	555	540	530
0	530	510	505
-5	500	500	500
-10 and lower	500	500	500

Percentile

When you take your actual SSAT exam, you will also receive a **percentile** ranking comparing your performance against the performance of other students of your gender and grade who have taken the SSAT within the past three years. For example, a percentile of 62 means that you scored higher than 62% of other SSAT test-takers of your gender and grade. Because your percentile ranking shows how well you performed according to your own grade level, these rankings are frequently given the most consideration by admissions offices.

The following chart provides an estimate of your SSAT percentile ranking based on your **raw scores** for this practice test. Keep in mind that the percentiles below are estimates only and are not specific to your own grade and gender. Because younger students are expected to score differently than older students on this exam, your percentile may be higher or lower than this estimate depending on your grade.

Upper Level Percentiles			
Raw Score	Math	Reading	Verbal
60			99
55			99
50	99		98
45	96		94
40	87	99	87
35	75	94	77
30	62	78	63
25	45	57	47
20	30	36	31
15	18	20	18
10	9	8	8
5	3	3	3
0	1	1	1
-5	1	1	1
-10 and lower	1	1	1

The following chart shows the median (50th percentile) **scaled scores** for each grade level. If you are scoring at the median for your grade level, this means that you scored higher than half of your peers.

Upper Level Median Scores			
Grade	Math	Reading	Verbal
Grade 8	676	647	660
Grade 9	699	653	667
Grade 10	705	659	670
Grade 11	704	647	656

Upper Level
Practice Test 4

Section 1 (Pages 181-188)

1. B	6. B	11. E	16. A	21. A
2. C	7. E	12. E	17. D	22. C
3. A	8. E	13. C	18. C	23. D
4. D	9. A	14. A	19. D	24. B
5. B	10. B	15. E	20. A	25. E

Section 2 (Pages 190-203)

1. C	9. D	17. B	25. B	33. B
2. B	10. D	18. D	26. D	34. E
3. E	11. E	19. D	27. E	35. C
4. A	12. A	20. B	28. D	36. A
5. C	13. A	21. A	29. C	37. D
6. E	14. C	22. A	30. A	38. C
7. A	15. B	23. C	31. B	39. E
8. E	16. A	24. B	32. A	40. B

Section 3 (Pages 204-211)

1. C	13. E	25. B	37. C	49. B
2. B	14. A	26. A	38. A	50. C
3. D	15. E	27. A	39. C	51. C
4. A	16. D	28. D	40. C	52. D
5. E	17. B	29. E	41. E	53. A
6. B	18. A	30. B	42. D	54. B
7. E	19. A	31. C	43. E	55. E
8. D	20. D	32. B	44. A	56. D
9. A	21. D	33. E	45. C	57. C
10. C	22. B	34. A	46. E	58. B
11. A	23. C	35. C	47. C	59. D
12. C	24. B	36. E	48. D	60. A

Section 4 (Pages 212-219)

1. A	6. C	11. B	16. B	21. A
2. C	7. D	12. E	17. A	22. B
3. D	8. E	13. C	18. D	23. E
4. D	9. A	14. B	19. C	24. D
5. C	10. D	15. B	20. E	25. E

Scoring Your Test

First, count up the number of questions you answered correctly, the number of questions you skipped, and the number of questions you answered incorrectly. Then, calculate your raw score using the following formula:

$$\text{Raw Score} = \text{\# of questions correct} - \frac{\text{\# of questions incorrect}}{4}$$

Add together your raw scores from your two math sections in order to determine your total raw math score.

Once you have found your raw score, convert it into an approximate scaled score using the estimated scoring charts on the next page. Keep in mind that you may score within 100 points of this estimate when you take your actual SSAT exam.

My Raw Score for Practice Test 4				
Section	# of Questions Correct	# of Questions Incorrect		Raw Score
Verbal	−	÷ 4	=	
Reading	−	÷ 4	=	
Math 1 + Math 2	−	÷ 4	=	

Scaled Score

Once you have found your raw score, convert it into an approximate **scaled score** using the scoring charts that follow. These charts provide an estimate for your SSAT scaled score based on your performance on this practice test. Keep in mind that your scaled score may differ within 100 points of this estimate when you take your actual SSAT exam, depending on the SSAT's specific scaling for that exam and any differences in your own test-taking process.

	Upper Level Scaled Scores		
Raw Score	Math	Reading	Verbal
60			800
55			800
50	800		780
45	780		750
40	755	800	725
35	725	720	700
30	700	690	645
25	670	660	645
20	640	630	615
15	615	600	590
10	585	570	565
5	555	540	530
0	530	510	505
-5	500	500	500
-10 and lower	500	500	500

Percentile

When you take your actual SSAT exam, you will also receive a **percentile** ranking comparing your performance against the performance of other students of your gender and grade who have taken the SSAT within the past three years. For example, a percentile of 62 means that you scored higher than 62% of other SSAT test-takers of your gender and grade. Because your percentile ranking shows how well you performed according to your own grade level, these rankings are frequently given the most consideration by admissions offices.

The following chart provides an estimate of your SSAT percentile ranking based on your **raw scores** for this practice test. Keep in mind that the percentiles below are estimates only and are not specific to your own grade and gender. Because younger students are expected to score differently than older students on this exam, your percentile may be higher or lower than this estimate depending on your grade.

Upper Level Percentiles			
Raw Score	Math	Reading	Verbal
60			99
55			99
50	99		98
45	96		94
40	87	99	87
35	75	94	77
30	62	78	63
25	45	57	47
20	30	36	31
15	18	20	18
10	9	8	8
5	3	3	3
0	1	1	1
-5	1	1	1
-10 and lower	1	1	1

The following chart shows the median (50th percentile) **scaled scores** for each grade level. If you are scoring at the median for your grade level, this means that you scored higher than half of your peers.

Upper Level Median Scores			
Grade	Math	Reading	Verbal
Grade 8	676	647	660
Grade 9	699	653	667
Grade 10	705	659	670
Grade 11	704	647	656

Made in the USA
Middletown, DE
25 June 2020